Self-Publishing

SELF-PUBLISHING FOR PROFIT, INNER FULFILLMENT AND SERVICE TO HUMANITY

HOW TO
SELF-PUBLISH YOUR BOOK
AND SAVE OVER 50%
OF THE COST OF A
PROFESSIONAL BOOK PRINTER
AND DISCOVER THE JOY OF
INNER FULFILLMENT, SELF-DISCOVERY
AND BRINGING
ENLIGHTENING IDEAS TO THE WORLD

C.M. Books
© 1998-1999-2000-2001-2002-2006

Self-Publishing

Cruzian Mystic Books
P. O. Box 570459
Miami, Fl. 33257
(305) 378-6253 Fax: (305) 378-6253

First U.S. edition 1997
©1998-1999-2000-2001
©2002-2006 By Reginald Muata Abhaya Ashby
All rights reserved. No part of this book may be used or reproduced in any manner whatsoever without written permission (address above) except in the case of brief quotations embodied in critical articles and reviews. All inquiries may be addressed to the address above.

The author is available for group lectures and individual counseling. For further information contact the publisher.

Ashby, Reginald M.
Self-publishing For Profit, Inner Fulfillment and Service to Humanity ISBN: 1-884564-40-2

Library of Congress Cataloging in Publication Data
1 Self Publishing

You can visit us on the World Wide Web
At
http://www.Egyptianyoga.com
E-MAIL ADDRESS: Semayoga@aol.com

Self-Publishing

Notice: Before you proceed with your printing job you should consult your printer or copy service to insure that all of your materials are properly formatted in order to avoid costly mistakes. The information provided in this manual is only intended as a guide and is not suitable for each and every job or for every person. The publishing of books requires a detail-oriented personality. There are many factors not covered in this booklet since these would go beyond the scope of this booklet. It is not intended as a technical manual but as an overview for understanding the process of producing your books yourself. Therefore, neither the author nor publisher of this booklet can assume responsibility for the success or failure of your project. You should also read the references provided below for more information on putting your project together.

Self-Publishing
Contents

Contents 4
Introduction..5

Introduction

Every time I go to a Book Expo, seminar or conference, I am always approached with the same question. How was I able to produce so many books in such a short time? Many people have wonderful ideas which they would like to bring forth, but they become frustrated due to lack of funds and lack of expertise in the area of Self-Publishing. Many think that the only way to get a book published is to go through the long and often disappointing process of submitting a manuscript to a professional publisher. We will refer to this as traditional publishing. Their ideas of Self-Publishing are also limited. Many believe they have to go through a traditional Commercial Book Printer and order at least 1,000 books at a time which will require several thousands of dollars. Otherwise, they go to copy stores where they pay 5¢, 10¢ or more per page and then get spiral or wire binding at $1.50 or more per book. Though this may not seem like much, it will add up to make the cost per book such that you will not be able to sell the books at a reasonable price and still make a profit. Also, most major bookstores do not want materials that are bound in such a fashion or presented with low quality copies. Thankfully, modern technology is getting simpler for everyone to use. It can be a great benefit to the small book publisher once he or she gets over the fear as to their own potential to learn and choose to embark on a road that will carry them into the future.

Self-Publishing

The intimidating fear of modern technology due to ignorance.

I introduced 10 new books in 1997, yet, I have limited funds. Printing an ordinary book containing 200 pages may require an investment of $2,500 or more using the traditional publishing method. Ten books would mean an investment of $25,000 or more. Yet, I was able to create a thriving publishing firm with a line of over 15 books which are sold in major bookstores all over the world, starting out with less than $5,000.

How was I able to do this? This is what I want to share with you through this booklet. This booklet is the result of my struggle and success in finding a way to produce the books that were in my mind, but could not find an outlet through the traditional publishing industry. You have an added advantage over me which will make more of your funds available for your books. You see, when I started out, I had no guide so I made lots of mistakes, some of them costly. You will benefit from my experiences. I hope that it will be enlightening and useful to you in bringing your ideas to the world through the art of literature.

Self-Publishing
The Philosophy of Publishing

What does "Righteous Self-publishing for Profit, Inner Fulfillment and Service to Humanity" mean? What is righteousness and how does it relate to publishing a book, inner fulfillment and service to humanity?

> "There are two roads traveled by humankind, those who seek to live MAAT, and those who seek to satisfy their animal passions."
>
> Ancient Egyptian Proverb

There are several books on self-publishing but none show how a person can use the new home computing technology to create top quality books without going to the traditional book printers which costs many thousands of dollars. The book shows how many books can be produced for the price of one. This book also introduces a new process of self-publishing which is revolutionary and which has not been available in the past until recently (last 4 years), due to the introduction of a new generation of machines which allow the possibility of circumventing the printing press. However, this book also introduces a new philosophy of publishing, which will lead the publisher to a spiritually and materially enriching career.

The book introduces a very important subject for our time, that is, publishing ideas that are useful to and needed by society instead of producing junk literature just to make money while putting out ideas and thoughts in literary form which will contribute to the further deg-

Self-Publishing

radation of society. If this principle is adhered to the publishing work will be both financially and spiritually rewarding. From what I have seen at book fairs, I think this topic is very important for people who want to publish their work. Also, there are many there that are frustrated at not being able to publish their work for lack of funds. As you will see, the cause of failure in various activities of life is not due to chance but due to a person's past actions, feelings and desires. If you study and apply the philosophy and techniques presented in this book you will succeed in your life not just professionally but spiritually as well. With our method anyone can publish a high quality book with less than $1000 dollars and distribute it around the world.

If you have read any of my other books you will know that I am a strong exponent of Yoga philosophy, especially the Yoga of Righteous Action. This is because I feel it is the path, which leads a person to discover true happiness in life. The practice of Yoga goes back to very ancient times. You may be asking why I am talking about Yoga Philosophy in a book about publishing? Well, Sages and Saints have written and published books from ancient times. In fact they were the first to write and publish books and their books stand today as immortal classics for all time. Why is that? First, you must understand that your actions in the world are not in a vacuum. They affect everyone else and eventually you will reap the consequences of your actions. So it is important to engage in good actions so as to reap the reward of mental peace and an enriching life. Yoga is the best path to accomplish this no matter what your chosen job, profession or career may be. In fact you were not placed on earth just to become rich, famous, etc. These things are fleeting and must eventually come to an end. A life of righteousness will allow you a chance to discover the true purpose and meaning of life, to discover happiness, which cannot be bought, true happiness, which cannot be stolen from you and which, is not dependent on your bank account. This form of happiness can only be discovered when a person's life is in harmony with the inner self and with the universe. Other-wise, even if you have millions in your account you may be so miserable as to kill yourself (see the head-lines of any newspaper or the TV tabloids).

What is Yoga Philosophy?

Since a complete treatise on the theory and practice of yoga would require several volumes, only a basic outline will be given here.

When we look out upon the world, we are often baffled by the multiplicity, which constitutes the human experience. What do we really know about this experience? Many scientific disciplines have developed over the last two hundred years for the purpose of discovering the mysteries of nature, but this search has only engendered new questions about the nature of existence. Yoga is a discipline or way of life de-signed to promote the physical, mental and spiritual development of the human being. It leads a person to discover the answers to the most important questions of life such as Who am I? Why am I here? and Where am I going?

The literal meaning of the word YOGA is to "*YOKE*" or to "*LINK*" back. The implication is: to link back to the original source, the original essence, that which transcends all mental and intellectual at-tempts at comprehension, but which is the essential nature of everything in CREATION. While in the strict or dogmatic sense, Yoga philosophy and practice is a separate discipline from religion, yoga and religion have been linked at many points throughout history. In a manner of speaking, Yoga as a discipline may be seen as a non-sectarian transpersonal science or practice to promote spiritual development and harmony of mind and body thorough mental and physical disciplines including meditation, psycho-physical exercises, and performing action with the correct attitude.

The disciplines of Yoga fall under five major categories. These are *Yoga of Wisdom, Yoga of Devotional Love, Yoga of Meditation, Tantric Yoga* and *Yoga of Selfless Action*. Within these categories there are subsidiary forms which are part of the main disciplines. The important point to remember is that all aspects of yoga can and should be used in an integral fashion to effect an efficient and harmonized spiritual movement in the practitioner. Therefore, while there may be an area of special emphasis, other elements are bound to become part of the yoga program as needed. For example, while a yogin may place emphasis on the yoga of wisdom, they may also practice devotional yoga and meditation yoga along with the wisdom studies.

While it is true that yogic practices may be found in religion, strictly speaking, yoga is neither a religion nor a philosophy. It should be thought of more as a way of life or discipline for promoting greater fullness and experience of life. Those who wanted more out of life developed yoga at the dawn of history. These special men and women wanted to discover the true origins of creation and of themselves. Therefore, they set out to explore the vast reaches of consciousness within themselves. They are sometimes referred to as "Seers", "Sages", etc. Awareness or consciousness can only be increased when the mind is in a state of peace and harmony. Thus, the disciplines of meditation (which are part of Yoga), and wisdom (the philosophical teachings for understanding reality as it is) are the primary means to controlling the mind and al-lowing the individual to mature psychologically and spiritually.

The teachings, which were practiced in the ancient Egyptian temples, were the same ones later intellectually defined into a literary form by the Indian Sages of Vedanta and Yoga. This was discussed in my book *Egyptian Yoga: The Philosophy of Enlightenment*. The Indian Mysteries of Yoga and Vedanta represent an unfolding and intellectual exposition of the Egyptian Mysteries. Also, the study of Gnostic Christianity or Christianity before Roman Catholicism will be useful to our study since Christianity originated in ancient Egypt and was also based on the ancient Egyptian Mysteries. Therefore, the study of the Egyptian Mysteries, early Christianity and Indian Vedanta-Yoga will provide the most comprehensive teaching on how to practice the disciplines of yoga leading to the attainment of Enlightenment.

The question is how to accomplish these seemingly impossible tasks? How to transform yourself and realize the deepest mysteries of existence? How to discover "who am I?" This is the mission of Yoga Philosophy and the purpose of yogic practices. Yoga does not seek to convert or impose religious beliefs on any one. Ancient Egypt was the source of civilization and the source of religion and Yoga. Therefore, all systems of mystical spirituality can coexist harmoniously within these teachings when they are correctly understood.

The goal of yoga is to promote integration of the mind-body-spirit complex in order to produce optimal health of the human being. This is accomplished through mental and physical exercises, which promote the free flow of spiritual energy by reducing mental complexes caused by ignorance. There are two roads which human beings can follow one of wisdom and the other of ignorance. The path of the masses is generally the path of ignorance, which leads them into negative situations, thoughts and deeds. These in turn lead to ill health and sorrow in life. The other road is based on wisdom and it leads to health, true happiness and enlightenment.

Yoga and Publishing

In ancient times (ancient Egypt) publishing was seen as a spiritual process of bringing forth the words of God into manifestation. Publishing is a way of self-expression and self-expression can be a path to spiritual expansion. However, all too often it is a venue for what is base and sensationalistic for the purpose of making money, or other egoistic ends and these lead a person to contraction, unfulfilment, stress and disease.

Self-Publishing

When publishing is done with the higher ideal in mind no matter what subject is chosen it will have a positive spiritual dimension and will be beneficial for all. If this ideal is not in mind the teachings of Maat (righteous philosophy) say that this work may be financially fruitful in the beginning but will lead to a spiritual deficit as well as discontent and frustration in life in the areas that are truly important.

Virtue, Righteousness, Karma and Purity of Heart

In order to understand what true virtue is and all of the elements that drive a human being and cause him or her to be the way he or she is, we must begin by understanding the teachings of karma and reincarnation. The human being is not simply a mind and body which will someday cease to exist. In fact, every human being's mind and body are in reality emanations or expressions of their eternal soul. The mind and body are referred to as the ego-personality, and it is this ego-personality which is temporal and mortal. The soul is immortal and perfect while the ego-personality is subject to error, confusion and the consequences of these. If a human being is aware of the deeper soul-reality, this state of being is known as the state of *Enlightenment*. However, if a human being does not have knowledge and experience of their Higher Self, then they exist in a condition of ignorance, which will lead to sinful behavior, pain and sorrow in life.

The ego-personality is subject to the forces of time and space and will suffer the consequences of its actions. This is the basis for the teaching of Karma. When the ego-personality dies, the soul moves on. If the human being has discovered his/her Higher Self (purified the heart (mind and body)), then the soul moves forward to unite with the supreme Self (God). If the ego in a person is fettered by ignorance, then the soul moves in an astral plane until it finds another ego-personality about to be born again in the world of time and space so that it may have an opportunity to have experiences that will lead it to discover its higher nature. This is the basis for the teaching of reincarnation.

"He delivers whom he pleases, even from the Duat (Netherworld)."
"He saves a man or woman from what is His lot at the dictates of their heart."

The utterances above are directly referring to Meskhent or karma. Many people believe that karma is equal to fate or destiny, however, this interpretation could not be further from the original understanding of the ancient Sages. The etymology of the word, karma, comes from the Sanskrit "karman" which means deed or action. In Yoga philosophy, karma also refers to one's actions and these same actions lead to certain experiences and consequences. In ancient Egyptian philosophy, the word Meskhent comes from the goddess who goes by the same name. She presides over the birth circumstances and life experiences of every individual. She is the one who carries out the decree, which has been ordained by Lord Djehuti after the judgment of the heart in the hall of MAAT. It is Lord Djehuti who records the deeds (actions) or karmas of every individual and then decrees what the Shai and Rennenet, which are fitting for that particular individual.

Self-Publishing
causes the individual to experience the proper circumstan

Then with the help of Shai and Rennenet, Meskhent The ancient Egyptian eroglyphic symbol of the heart is a heart shaped vase, ০ৡ The vase is a container, which may be used for water, beer, wine, milk, etc. Likewise, the human heart is seen as a vessel, which contains thoughts, feelings, desires and unconscious memories. In mystical terms, the heart is a metaphor of the human mind including the conscious, subconscious and unconscious levels. The mind is the reservoir of all of your ideas, convictions and feelings. There-fore, just as these factors direct the path of your life, so too they are the elements, which are judged in the Hall of Maati by the two goddesses, Isis and Nephthys, along with Osiris. The heart then is the sum total of your experiences, actions and aspirations, your con-science or karma, and these are judged in the balance against the feather of Maat.

Thus, karma should be thought of as the total effect of a person's actions and conduct during the successive phases of his/her existence. But how does this effect operate? How do the past actions affect the present and the future? Your experiences from the present life or from previous lifetimes cause unconscious impressions, which stay with the Soul even after death. These unconscious impressions are what constitute the emerging thoughts, desires, and aspirations of every individual. These impressions are not exactly like memories, however, they work like memories. For example, if you had a fear in a previous lifetime or the childhood of your present lifetime, you

Self-Publishing

may not remember the event that caused the fear, but

Self-Publishing

you may experience certain phobias when you come into contact with certain objects or certain people. These feelings are caused by the unconscious impressions, which are coming up to the surface of the conscious mind. It is this conglomerate of unconscious impressions which are "judged" in the Hall of MAAT and determine where the soul will go to next in the spiritual journey toward evolution or devolution, also known as the cycle of birth and death or reincarnation, as well as the experiences of heaven or hell. The following segment from the ancient Egyptian "Instruction to Mer-ka-Ré" explains this point.

> *"You know that they are not merciful the day when they judge the miserable one ....Do not count on the passage of the years; they consider a lifetime as but an hour. After death man remains in existence and His acts accumulate beside him. Life in the other world is eternal, but he who arrives without sin before the Judge of the Dead, he will be there as a Neter and he will walk freely as do the masters of eternity."*

The reference above to "His acts accumulate beside him" alludes to the unconscious impressions, which are formed as a result of one's actions while still alive. These impressions can be either positive or negative. Positive impressions are developed through positive actions by living a life of righteousness (MAAT) and virtue. This implies living according to the precepts of mystical wisdom or being a follower of Horus *(Shemsu Hor)* and Isis. These actions draw one closer to harmony and peace, thus paving the way to discover the Self within. The negative impressions are developed through sinful actions. They are related to mental agitation, disharmony and restlessness. This implies acts based on anger, fear, desire, greed, depression, gloom, etc. These actions draw one into the outer world of human desires. They distract the mind and do not allow the intellect (Saa) to function. Thus, existence at this level is closer to an animal, being based on animal instincts and desires of the body (selfishness), rather than to a spiritually mature human being, being based on reason, selflessness, compassion, etc.

(Purification of the heart)

How then is it possible to eradicate negative karmic impressions and to develop positive ones? The answer lies in your understanding of the wisdom teachings and your practice of them. When you study the teachings and live according to them, your mind undergoes a transformation at all levels. This transformation is the "purification of heart" so often spoken about throughout the *Egyptian Book of Coming Forth by Day*. It signifies an eradication of negative impressions, which renders the mind pure and subtle. When the mind is rendered subtle, then spiritual realization is possible. This discipline of purifying the heart by living according to the teachings is known as the Yoga of Action or MAAT.

The philosophy of MAAT is a profound teaching, which encompasses the fabric of creation as well as a highly effective system of spiritual discipline. In creation stories, God (Neter Neteru) is said to have established creation upon MAAT. Consequently it follows that MAAT is the orderly flow of energy which maintains the universe. Further, MAAT is the regularity which governs the massive planetary and solar systems as well as the growth of a blade of grass and a human cell. This natural process represents the flow of creation wherein there is constant movement and a balancing of opposites (up-down, hot-cold, here-there, you-me, etc.).

Most people act out of the different forces, which are coursing through them at the time. These may be hunger, lust, fear, hatred, anger, elation, etc. They have no control over these because they have not understood that their true essence is in reality separate from their thoughts and emotions. They have *identified* with their thoughts and therefore are led to the consequences of those thoughts and the deeds they engender. You, as an aspirant, having developed a higher level of spiritual sensitivity, are now aware that you have a choice in the thoughts you think and the actions you perform. You can choose whether to act in ways that are in harmony with MAAT or those that are disharmonious. You have now studied the words of wisdom and must now look beyond the level of ritual worship of the Divine to the realm of practice and experience of the Divine.

In ordinary human life, those who have not achieved the state of Enlightenment (the masses in society at large) perceive nature as a conglomeration of forces which are unpredictable and in need of control. However, as spiritual sensitivity matures, the aspirant realizes that what once appeared to be chaotic is in reality the Divine Plan of the Supreme Being in the process of unfoldment. When this state of consciousness is attained, the aspirant realizes that there is an underlying order in nature, which can only be perceived with spiritual eyes.

The various injunctions of MAAT are for the purpose of keeping order in society among ordinary people, people without psychological maturity and, or spiritual sensitivity, meaning that they lack an awareness of spiritual principles and moral - ethical development. Also, they provide insight into the order of creation and a pathway or spiritual discipline, which when followed, will lead the aspirant to come into harmony with the cosmic order. When the individual attunes his or her own sense of order and balance with the cosmic order, a spontaneous unity occurs between the individual and the cosmos, and the principles of MAAT, rather than being a blind set of rules which we must strive to follow, become a part of one's inner character and proceed from one in a spontaneous manner.

This means that through the deeper understanding of cosmic order and by the practice of living in harmony with that order, the individual will lead him or herself to mental and spiritual peace and harmony. It is this peace and harmony, which allows the lake of the mind to become a clear mirror in which the individual soul is able to realize its oneness with the Universal Soul.

Self-Publishing
MAAT as the Spiritual Path of Righteous Action

MAAT is equivalent to the Chinese concept of the *Tao* or *"The Way"* of nature. This *"Way"* of nature, from the *Tao-te-Ching,* the main text of Taoism, represents the harmony of human and Divine (universal) consciousness. Also, MAAT may be likened with the Indian idea of *Dharma* or the ethical values of life and the teachings related to *Karma Yoga,* the yogic spiritual discipline which emphasizes selfless service and the attitude that actions are being performed by God who is working through you instead of your personal ego-self. God is working through you to serve humanity, which is also essentially God. All Buddhist Monks utter the prayer *I go to the Buddha for refuge. I go to the Dharma for refuge. I go to the monastic order for refuge.*

The Buddhist aspirant is admonished to take refuge in the *Buddha* (one's innate *Buddha Consciousness),* the *Dharma,* and the *Sanga* (company of en-lightened personalities). The following statement from chapter 9 of the Bhagavad Gita shows how Lord Krishna admonished his followers to seek sanctuary in him as Jesus did hundreds of years later.

32. O Arjuna, those who take refuge in Me

Jesus also exhorted his followers to bring him their troubles "and He will give them rest". Dharma is understood as the spiritual discipline based on righteousness, order and truth, which sustains the universe. In the same way, the ancient Egyptian Initiate was to lean upon MAAT in order to purify his or her heart so as to uncover the virtuous character which leads to Divine awareness.

> "There are two roads traveled by humankind, those who seek to live MAAT, and those who seek to satisfy their animal passions."
>
> -Ancient Egyptian Proverb

It is important here to gain a deeper understanding of what is meant by *action*. In primeval times, before creation, the primordial ocean existed in complete peace and rest. When that ocean was agitated with the first thought of God, the first *act* was performed. Through the subsequent *acts of mind* or *eforts of divine thought,* creation unfolded in the form of the various gods and goddesses who form the "companies of Gods". They represent the qualities of nature (hot-cold, wet-dry, etc.) in the form of pairs of opposites. When the first primeval thought emerged from the primeval ocean of pure potentiality, immediately there was something other than the single primordial essence. Now there is a being who is looking and perceiving the rest of the primordial essence. This is the origin of duality in the world of time and space and the triad of human consciousness. Instead of there being one entity, there appears to be two. The perception instrument, the mind and senses, is the third factor, which comprises the triad. Therefore, while you consider yourself to be an individual, you are in reality one element in a triad which all together comprise the content of your human experiences. There is a perceiver (the real you), that which is being perceived (the object) and the act of perception itself (through the mind and

Self-Publishing

senses).

Self-Publishing

With this first primordial act, God set into motion events, which operate according to regular and ceaseless motion or action. This is the foundation upon which the universe is created and it emerges from the mind of God. Therefore, if one is able to think and act according to the way in which God thinks and acts, then there will be oneness with God. Human beings are like sparks of divine consciousness, and as such, are endowed with free will to act in any given way. This free will, when dictated by the egoism of the individual mind, causes individual human beings to feel separate from God. This delusion of the mind leads it to develop ideas related to its own feelings and desires. These egoistic feelings and desires lead to the performance of egoistic acts in an effort to satisfy those perceived needs and desires. This pursuit of fulfillment of desires in the relative world of the mind and senses leads the soul to experience pain, sorrow and frustration, because these can never be 100% satisfied. Frustration leads to more actions in search of fulfillment.

The fleeting feelings, which most people have associated with happiness and passion, are only ephemeral glimpses of the true happiness and peace, which can be experienced if the source of true fulfillment within you was to be discovered. MAAT shows a way out of the pain and sorrow of human existence and leads you to discover Osiris within you, the source of eternal bliss and supreme peace. If you choose to act according to your own will (ego), then you will be in contradiction with MAAT. This means that you are contradicting your own conscience, creating negative impressions which will become lodged in the heart (unconscious mind) and will cause continuous mental agitation while you are alive and hellish experiences for yourself after death. The negative impressions rise up at given times in the form of uncontrolled desires, cravings, unrest, and the other forms of self-torment with which human life abounds.

It is important to understand that when the soul is attuned to a physical body, mind and senses, the experiences occur through these. Thus, the experiences of pleasure and pain are regulated by how much the body, mind and senses can take. If there is too much pain the body faints. When there is too much pleasure the mind and senses become weakened and swoons into unconsciousness or sleep. If there is too much pleasure, there develops elation and the soul is carried off with the illusion of pleasure, which creates a longing and craving for more and more in an endless search for fulfillment.

However, after death, there is no safety valve as it were. Under these conditions the soul will have the possibility of experiencing boundless amounts of pleasure or pain according to its karmic basis. This is what is called heaven and hell, respectively. Therefore, if you have lived a balanced life (MAAT), then you will not have the possibility of experiencing heaven or hell. Rather, you will retain presence of mind and will not fall into the delusion of ignorance. Therefore, the rewards of developing a balanced mind during life continues after death. This mental equanimity allows you to see the difference between the truth and the illusions of the mind and senses, in life as well as in death.

Thus, if you choose to act in accordance with MAAT, you will be in a position to transcend the egoistic illusions of the mind and thereby become free from the vicious cycle of actions, which keep the mind, tied to its illusory feelings and desires. When the mind is freed from the "vicious cycle", the soul's bondage to the world of time and space is dissolved because it is not being controlled by the mind but has become the controller of the mind. When the practice of MAAT is perfected, the mind becomes calm. When this occurs, the ocean of consciousness, which was buffeted by the stormy winds of thoughts, anxieties, worries and desires, becomes calm. This calmness allows the soul to cease its identification with the thoughts of the mind and to behold its true nature as a separate entity from the mind, senses, feelings and thoughts of the ego-self. The soul is now free to expand its vision beyond the constrictive pettiness of human desires and mental agitation, in order to behold the expansion of the inner Self.

Actions are the basis upon which the Cosmic Plan of creation unfolds. In human life, it is the present action, which leads to the results that follow at some point in the future, in this life or in another lifetime. Therefore, if you are in a prosperous situation today or an adverse one, it is because of actions you performed in the past. Thus, both situations, good or bad, should be endured with a sense of personal responsibility and equanimity of mind (MAAT). From a transcendental point of view, the Soul looks at all situations equally. This is because the Soul knows itself to be immortal and eternal, and untouched by the events of human existence, which it has witnessed for countless lifetimes. It is the ego, which is transient, that looks on life situations as pressing and real and therefore either tries to hold onto situations which it considers to be "good" or to get away from or eradicate situations which it considers to be "bad". All situations, whether they are considered to be good or bad by the ego, will eventually pass on, so we should try to view them as clouds which inevitably pass on, no matter how terrible or how wonderful they may seem to be. When life is lived in this manner, the mind develops a stream of peace, which rises above elation and depression, prosperity and adversity. By looking at situations with equal vision and doing your best regardless of the circumstances, you are able to discover an unalterable balance within yourself. This is MAAT, the underlying order and truth behind the apparent chaos and disorder in the phenomenal world. In doing this, you are able to attune your mind to the cosmic mind of the innermost Self, which exists at that transcendental level of peace all the time.

This means that if you are, deep down, indeed the Universal Self, one with God, and if you have come to your current situation in life of bondage to the world of time and space due to your own state of mental ignorance, then it follows that if you undertake certain disciplines of knowledge (studying the teachings) and daily practice (following the teachings), those same actions will lead you to liberation from the state of bondage. Ignorance of your true Self is the root cause of your bondage to the karmic cycle of life-death-reincarnation-life-death-reincarnation, etc.

Self-Publishing

Everyone must perform actions. Even breathing is an action. Therefore, nobody can escape actions. No one can say: "I will go far away from civilization and escape all actions and then my actions will not lead me to a state of ignorance about my true Self". This form of thinking is a fallacy because, as just discussed, breathing, eating, drinking, sleeping, sitting, and walking are actions. The process of liberation requires more than just removing yourself from the field of physical actions. You could go to a quiet cave, temple or church and you would still be plagued by the unruly thoughts of the mind which cause distraction from the Self. Thoughts are subtle forms of actions. Therefore, an action performed in thought can be equally significant and cause as much karmic entanglement as an action performed with the body. An action first originates in the mental field (astral plane) of consciousness, which is stirred by desires rising from the unconscious mind. This agitation prompts the mind toward thoughts and actions in an attempt to fulfill the desires of the unconscious, but those actions and thoughts create more desires and more future agitation. This is the state of bondage, which is experienced by most people, and it continues for lifetimes without end. This cycle continues until there is a discovery that desires cannot be fulfilled in this manner. Therefore, the root of desire, ignorance, must be eradicated in order to end the desires of the mind and achieve true peace and balance.

You need to develop subtlety of intellect and profound insight into the nature of the universe and of your innermost Self. The best way to achieve this goal is to practice a blending of wisdom and action in your personal spiritual discipline in order to harmonize your mental and physical qualities.

In this process, you must understand that the ancient Sages have given guidelines for which thoughts and actions are in line with the scales of MAAT, and which actions and thoughts are not. The 42 precepts of MAAT constitute the focus of the Egyptian Book of Coming Forth By Day, however, throughout the book, many injunctions are given. Their purpose is to cleanse the heart of the aspirant.

"The wise person who acts with MAAT is free of falsehood and disorder."

Ancient Egyptian Proverb

The practice of MAAT signifies *wisdom in action*. This is to say that the teachings are to be practiced in ordinary day to day situations, and when the deeper implications of this practice are understood, one will be led to purity in action and thought.

In order to become one with the Divine, you must become the Divine in thought and deed. This means that you must spiritualize your actions and your thoughts at all times and under all conditions. Actions which present themselves to you in the normal course of the day, as well as those actions which you have planned for the future, should be evaluated by your growing intellectual discerning quality, and then performed to your best capacity in a selfless manner.

Adversity in Life

Why is there adversity in life? Wouldn't it be nice if there was no misfortune or unluckiness to hamper your movement in life? Human life abounds with adversity. Even the very rich experience adversity. In fact, no matter who you are you will experience adversity of one form or another as you progress through life.

Adversity is a divine messenger. Imagine how life would be if you could do anything you wanted to do. You would indulge every desire and whim. You would only seek to satisfy your desire for pleasure and you would not accomplish anything significant in life. In the end you would be frustrated and disappointed because no matter how hard you try, it is not possible to ever completely satisfy your desires for the pleasures of the senses.

Adversity is a form of resistance which life places on all beings for the purpose of engendering in them a need to strive to overcome it. When adversity is met with the correct understanding and with the right attitude, it can become a great source of strength and spiritual inspiration. However, if adversity makes you hardhearted, insensitivity, selfish, cold and bitter, then you will lead yourself deeper into the quagmire of negativity and pain. Adversity is God's way of calling your attention away from negative ways of life and to draw attention toward the basic elements of life. Often when people succeed in acquiring some object they desired, they develop conceit and vanity. They look down on others and feel proud of their accomplishment. However, when they lose what they desired, they fall into the valley of adversity, despair, violence and anger. They blame others for their misfortune and seek to hurt others for their loss.

Many of those people who have experienced the most adversity in history include Sages and Saints. Why should God allow those who are trying to be closest to the Divine be plagued with adversity? The answer lies in an ancient Egyptian proverb:

> "Adversity is the seed of well doing; it is the nurse of heroism and boldness; who that hath enough, will endanger himself to have more? Who that is at ease, will set their life on the hazard?
>
> Ancient Egyptian Proverb

Have you noticed that it seems as though the people who are most righteous and deserving of prosperity are the ones who suffer the most in life? In families, the child who is most obedient gets the most attention and disciplinary control. People who are loving and compassionate suffer illnesses and pain from others. This is because nature has been set up by God to create situations which challenge human beings so as to provide for them opportunities to discover their inner resources which give them the capacity to overcome the trouble, and thereby grow in discovery of their deeper Self. Those who suffer most are in reality those who have drawn more attention from the Divine, indeed, chosen for more intense spiritual testing. This testing process of nature allows every soul the opportunity to face trouble with either boldness and faith or with fear and negativity. The rewards of adversity faced

Self-Publishing

well are increased strength of will and an increased feeling of discovery of the Divine within. When adversity is faced with negativity and ignorance, it leads to pain, sorrow and more adversity.

Therefore, adversity cannot be understood and successfully faced with negativity (anger, hatred, hardheartedness, etc.). Adversity can only be overcome with wisdom and virtue, and virtue is the first and most important quality to be developed by all serious spiritual aspirants.

From a spiritual perspective, what is considered to be prosperity by the masses of ignorant people is in reality adversity and what is considered to be adversity by the masses is in reality, prosperity. The masses consider that becoming rich and being able to indulge the pleasures of the senses through food, drink, drugs and sex is the ultimate goal, yet is there anyone who has discovered true peace and contentment because of billions of dollars? Having the opportunity to indulge the pleasures of the senses creates an opportunity for the mind to become more dependent on the worldly pleasures. This process intensifies the egoistic feelings and draws the soul away from discovering true peace within. There is increasing agitation and worry over gaining what is desired and then preoccupation with how to hold onto it. Not realizing that all must be left behind at the time of death, people keep on seeking worldly fame, fortune and glory, and in the process never discover true happiness. They have duped themselves into believing that material wealth brings happiness, because the greedy corporations,

Self-Publishing

the media and popular culture reinforce this message. In reality it is a philosophy of ignorance based on lack of reflection and spiritual insight. Adversity is a call to wake up from this delusion of pain and sorrow and those who are experiencing the worst conditions are receiving the loudest call. Therefore, adversity is in reality prosperity because it stimulates the mind through suffering so that it may look for a higher vision of life and discover the abode of true happiness, peace and contentment which transcends worldly measure.

This exalted vision of life is the innate potential of every human being. What is necessary is the dedication and perseverance to seek a higher understanding of the divine nature of creation and the divine nature of the innermost heart. It has the power to absolve and redeem all negativity. This is the highest goal of all human beings and the most difficult. However, as you gain greater understanding and greater will to act with virtue, your vision of the divine will increase and draw you closer and closer to the Higher Self. This is the glory of virtue and its power to vanquish and eradicate vice from the human heart.

Where Does True Happiness Come From?

In reality, happiness does not and cannot come from objects that can be acquired or from activities that are performed. It can only come from within. Even actions that seem to be pleasurable in life cannot be considered as a source of happiness from a philosophical point of view, because all activities are relative. This means that one activity is pleasurable for one person and painful for another. This leads to the realization that it is not the activity itself that holds the happiness, but the individual doer who is performing the action and assigning a value to it which she or he has learned from society or past karmic mental impressions to assign. Therefore, if it was learned that going out to a party is supposed to be fun, then that activity will be pursued as a source of happiness. Here action is performed in pursuit of the fruit of the action in the form happiness; a result is desired from the action. However, there are several negative psychological factors, which arise that will not allow true happiness to manifest. The first is that the relentless pursuit of the action renders the mind restless and agitated. The second is that if the activity is not possible, there will be depression in the mind. If the activity is thwarted by some outside force, meaning that something or someone prevented you from achieving the object or activity you saw as the "source of happiness," you develop anger towards it. If by chance you succeed in achieving the object or activity you become elated. This will cause greed in the mind and you will want more and more of it. When you are not able to get more at any particular time, you will become depressed and disappointed. Therefore, under these conditions, a constant dependence on outside activities and worldly objects develops in the mind, which will not allow for peace and contentment. Even though it is illogical to pursue activities which cause pain in life, people are constantly acting against their own interests as they engage in actions in an effort to gain happiness, while in reality, they are enhancing the probability of encountering pain later on. People often act and shortly thereafter, regret what they have done. Sometimes people know even at the time of their actions that they are wrong, and yet they are unable to stop themselves. This is because when desires and expectations control the mind, the intellect, the light of reason, is *clouded* and *dull*. However, when the mind is controlled by the intellect, then it is not possible to be led astray due to the *fantasies* and *illusions* of the mind. When the individual is guided by their purified intellect, only right actions can be performed no matter what negative ideas arise in the mind. Such a person cannot be deluded into negative actions, and when negative actions (actions which lead to future pain and disappointments) are not performed, unhappiness cannot exist. Thus, a person who lives according to the teachings of non-doership (perform action without desires or expectations for the future results of their actions) lives a life of perpetual peace and happiness in the present.

Thus, true peace and inner fulfillment will never come through pursuit of actions when there is an expectation or desire for the fruits of those actions. The belief in objects or worldly activities as a source of happiness is therefore seen as a state of *ignorance* wherein the individual is caught up in the *illusions, fantasies* and *fanciful notions* of the mind. However, happiness and peace can arise spontaneously when there is an attitude of detachment and dispassion towards objects and situations in life. If actions are performed with the idea of discovering peace within, based on the understanding of the philosophy outlined above, and for the sake of the betterment of society, then these actions will have the effect of purifying the heart of the individual. The desires and expectations will dwindle while the inner fulfillment and awareness of the present moment will increase. There will be greater and greater discovery of peace within, a discovery of what is truly stable and changeless within as opposed to the mind and outer world which are constantly changing and unpredictable.

Ancient Egyptian Proverbs On Righteousness in Business and Commerse from Sage Amenemope

> Do not assess a man who has nothing, And thus falsify your pen. If you find a large debt against a poor man, Make it into three parts; Forgive two, let one stand, You will find it a path of life. Haste not to be rich, but be not slothful in thine own interest. One does not run to reach success, One does not move to spoil it.

Keeping The Balance

> "Neither let prosperity put out the eyes of circumspection, nor abundance cut off the hands of frugality; they that too much indulge in the superfluities of life, shall live to lament the want of its necessaries."
> "See that prosperity elate not thine heart above measure; neither adversity depress thine mind unto the depths, because fortune beareth hard against you. Their smiles are not stable, therefore build not thy confidence upon them; their frowns endure not forever, therefore let hope teach you patience."
> Ancient Egyptian Proverbs

As the proverbs above suggest, equanimity is one of the most important qualities that a spiritual aspirant must develop in order to practice virtuous living. Vir-

Self-Publishing

tuous living requires strength of will because life is constantly tempting the mind and body toward the pleasures of the senses and toward egoistic desires. When the mind is constantly agitated, swinging back and forth becoming elated and exuberant in prosperous conditions and angry and agitated during adversity the mental energy is drained and dispersed. It becomes hard to concentrate, to act with clarity to distinguish between right and wrong and it becomes more difficult to fulfill the duties of life. This is why in the Egyptian Book of Coming Forth By Day the initiate is constantly saying that he or she *"Kept the Balance"* and is worthy to enter into the divine realms.

Undue mental agitation is the source of angry thoughts wherein people say and do things they would not otherwise do and get caught up in a patter wherein they are easily provoked by others who can "push the right buttons" which can anger them. When the mind is in control and always aware of the thoughts within as well as the world outside it is impossible for this mind to fall prey to the provocation of others or to despair or fear. This is the ideal of equanimity that is to be reached by living a virtuous life through the study and practice of the teachings of mystical spirituality.

> *"No one reaches the beneficent West unless their heart is righteous by doing MAAT. There is no distinction made between the inferior and the superior person; it only matters that one is found faultless when the balances and the two weights stand before the Lord of Eternity. No one is free from the reckoning.*

Self-Publishing

Djehuti, a baboon, holds the balances to count each one according to what they have done upon earth."

Ancient Egyptian Proverb

Below: Ancient Egyptian Scribes, the first publishers in history

 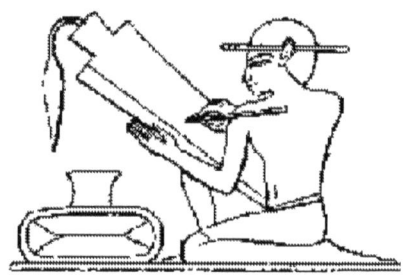

Seek Purity of Heart through an Attitude of Selfless Service:

Always keep in mind that you are performing actions with the grace of God, no matter what actions you perform. God is acting through you to uphold the order of the universe. You are the instrument of the Divine by which the he/she performs actions. Therefore, as you consciously attune yourself to MAAT, you are assisting in the support and positive evolution of the universe. Always keep in mind that as an aspirant, your soul, God, is leading you to certain experiences that are needed for your mental growth. Regardless of your situation, be it an adverse or prosperous situation, remember that your goal is to purify your heart so as to come into balance with the cosmic order of the Supreme Being, MAAT. You will realize that many situations which ordinary people, the masses, consider to be adversities, accidents, misfortunes, losses, etc. are in reality opportunities for you to practice your understanding of the teachings and control your ego-personality.

Whatever the situation is that presents itself to you, remember the divine intent behind it and offer your actions in response to it as an oblation or as a presentation made to the Divine as an act of worship. Each time that you remember the Divine throughout the normal course of a day, it is like taking a trip to a temple or holy site. When you offer your actions to the Divine and accept no egoistic credit for the actions, it is an even higher form of worship of the Divine. When you inwardly take the attitude that it is in reality the Divine Self who is acting and not you, this is the highest form of worship of the Divine. If you were able to maintain this form of awareness continuously you would achieve spiritual realization in a short time.

All things are in reality a manifestation of the Divine. Just as a candle's light and heat are one and the same, the manifestation (universe) and the Divine Self are one and the same. Therefore, the idea that there are individuals acting independently as various people with different names is an illusion backed up by mental ignorance. You must continue to assert this truth at all times in order to combat that ignorance and thereby purify your heart.

Seek Purity of Heart by Not Expecting a Reward For Your Actions

In performing your actions, never seek an external reward. Always feel that you are performing actions for the Divine Self in an effort to purify your heart of egoistic feelings and sentiments. External expectations and rewards for your actions are always bound to be fleeting and cannot be counted on. Therefore, if you base your happiness on something that is fleeting, you are basing it on an illusion, which will certainly lead to disappointment and unrest. Remember the definition of reality: that which is unchanging. Seek deep within you for what is unchanging regardless of the external situations. Seek for the eternal witnessing Self within you who is separate from the thoughts and transitory situations of the external world. Perform your actions well but do not become attached to them as sources of your happiness.

"They who revere MAAT are long lived; they who are covetous have no tomb."
Ancient Egyptian Proverb

In reality, it is the soul within you that gives meaning and worth to all externalities. Therefore, your soul is the source of all understanding, meaning and awareness. This soul is full of immense happiness (bliss) and you can discover this inward peace and happiness by inwardly discovering your true Self and not seeking happiness from objects outside of yourself. Seeking happiness and the fulfillment of desires through worldly pursuits and relationships only lead to frustrations and more desires. This constant fan-

Self-Publishing

ning of the waves of the mind with the thoughts of desires and cravings survives in the innermost recesses of the unconscious mind, embedded deep within the astral and causal bodies of the human being. These deep karmic impressions in the unconscious mind, which remain after the death of the physical body, lead the soul to astral heavens and hells, and to future embodiments in physical form.

The Ancient
Egyptian Goddess of Scribes:

Sesheta

Self-Publishing

Seek Purity of Heart Through Your Work Occupation and Daily Activities:

> *"Do not disturb a great person or distract their attention when they are occupied, trying to understand their task. When they are thus occupied they strip their body through love of what they do. Love for the work, which they do, brings people closer to God. These are the people who succeed in what they do."*
>
> Ancient Egyptian Proverb

Another profound insight into the teachings of MAAT is that you should always strive to perform work that is in harmony with your nature. As an expression of the Divine Self, you are endowed with unlimited capabilities and you should not allow your fears or the desires of others to limit the unfoldment of those energies. You must strive to allow yourself to gradually develop a sense of what is right for you. This occurs when you begin to develop peace and harmony within yourself. You will discover which jobs to pursue on the basis of your inner desire, rather than the superficial desire of your ego-self, which wants to pursue a job or occupation because it looks glamorous or lucrative.

Ancient Egyptian civilization placed high importance on the occupation of the individual due to these very reasons. Many people suffer through life because they have made the wrong choices about their chosen profession or occupation and feel stuck and unable to change their lot in life. Sometimes they are led by their families, or their own greed or fear, into pursuing occupations for the wrong reasons. You must understand that if you choose an occupation or career just to make money or because you have been told that some particular profession is in demand, etc., you may make some money at it but you will end up being miserable and disappointed with the work you have chosen as well as your life in general. Your career will truly become "work". It will not be fulfilling because you are not doing it out of the goodness of your heart. Eventually, it will become a struggle and a burden. Also, you will not develop divine qualities and mental peace, which will lead you toward Enlightenment, such as patience, contentment, forgiveness universal love, compassion, etc. Rather, your ego (ignorant and disturbed state of mind) will become more hardened and you will use unrighteous means to make money so that you can make money. You may sell things to people even though you know they do not need them or deal in products, which you know are harmful. All the while, your intellect, which is dulled by the desires, cravings and longings of the lower mind and senses for egoistic pleasures, will justify the unrighteous actions. However, the impressions of longing and desire as well as the contradictions of your own conscience become registered in the deep unconscious and create a basis for heaven or hell on earth as well as beyond. This is a profound teaching, which you need to reflect upon seriously.

Even though people who live and acquire wealth in this "Setian" manner seem happy with the wealth, in reality there is unrest in their "hearts" (minds). In fact, most people have been convinced that wealth is or brings happiness and this is the view of ignorance promoted by society at large and the media. While there is nothing wrong with having spiritual and material wealth, most people who are ignorant of spiritual truths become dependent and attached to their wealth as a source of pleasure and happiness and are therefore, bound to pursue, hoard and protect their wealth in order to be happy. However, this happiness which requires continued mental agitation and worry is no happiness at all. Even if you develop a prosperous situation for yourself, your worries and anxieties will not protect you from addictions, cravings and other forms of pain, which the world abounds with. Therefore, happiness, and consequently true wealth, is not to be found in objects or possessions of the world. It is a state of mind, which can be discovered through spiritual insight.

The impressions lodged in the unconscious mind form a storehouse of restless desires, which will lead to repeated embodiments and deprive you from discovering the peace of your Self.

Thus, while there seems to be little justice in the world, no deed goes unseen by MAAT who is the Self, the all-seeing Soul who supports all human activity and the cosmos. This Self is your very own innermost essence, therefore, you are essentially MAAT. You are the judge and jury of your own actions. Since you are ultimately the controller of your own actions as well as the judge of them, you can change your entire being by learning the ways of MAAT and eradicating the negativity and ignorance you have built up in this lifetime as well as the previous ones. This can

Self-Publishing

be accomplished by following the teachings outlined in the scriptures. Before blindly moving into worldly actions examine yourself first.

Ask yourself: *Do I need this relationship or this object or is it just to satisfy my ego's desire for lust, pleasure or greed? Is this action I am about to do going to help me simplify my life or will it complicate it more? Will it bring peace of mind or will it cause more agitation?* If it is for the ego it is a waste of time because the ego cannot be satisfied since it is an end-less pit of desire!

This process of introspection and self-awareness begins to break the cycle of actions performed out of weak will and ignorance, which lead to pain and sorrow later on.

The Ancient
Egyptian God of Scribes, *Djehuti,* in the form of an Ibis headed man and a baboon.

Self-Publishing

Choosing an occupation:

Many people are afraid to choose some occupation which is what they would really like to be doing because they fear where their next meal will come from, how they will be supported, etc. But didn't Jesus say:

> Matthew *6:28 And why are ye anxious for raiment? Consider the lilies of the field, how they grow; they toil not, neither do they spin:*
> *29 And yet I say to you, That even Solomon in all his glory was not arrayed like one of these.*
> *30 Wherefore, if God so clotheth the grass of the field, which to day is, and to morrow is cast into the oven, [shall he] not much more [clothe] you, O ye of little faith?*

This teaching exists in all major world philosophies. The task of the aspirant is to go beyond the fears of human existence. This is done by adopting the study of spiritual teachings and reflecting upon them with the assistance of the spiritual preceptor. Gradually, you will discover an occupation that resonates with your internal feeling. You will find something that you would do even if you were not paid. When this happens you will not be motivated by selfish motives and the work itself will be rewarding to you and to society. You will begin to discover a form of peace, which is not achieved by most people. This will assist you to have a peaceful disposition, which will allow you to progress further in your spiritual discipline. So don't worry, you

Self-Publishing

are a child of the universe and when you tread the path of spiritual aspiration, even though it may be difficult at some times, you will be provided for. This is a spiritual law. The key is continued effort in your spiritual discipline. Strive to understand the teachings no matter how many times you fail. Gradually incorporate meditation, recitations of words of power, study of the scriptures and remembrance of the divine through-out the day and you will be led to works which are in harmony with your nature.

Seek Purity of Heart Through Living a Life of Simplicity

> "When opulence and extravagance are a necessity instead of righteousness and truth, society will be governed by greed and injustice."
> Ancient Egyptian Proverb

The key to reducing worldly entanglements and negative karmic impressions, which will lead to future pain and reincarnation, is to reduce the desires in the mind. One important way to accomplish this is to simplify one's life. This implies reducing one's karmic entanglements and worries, which constantly agitate the mind. We are indoctrinated into believing that material wealth brings happiness, so much so that having achieved a measure of success, according to societal standards, we convince ourselves that we are happy, sometimes even if it means an early grave due to overwork and increased stress attempting to support luxuries which are not needed or pursuing ideals which are wrong for us. Many who may not have the material wealth are as if hypnotized by the idea that they "must" pursue it and once achieved, it will yield the long sought after happiness. Despite the disappointments and frustrations, we continue to pursue the dream, not realizing that material wealth does not automatically produce happiness. Further, if those who have achieved the riches are happy, it is not because of the riches but due to a much deeper psychological integration that has occurred. Also, just as the presence of material wealth does not necessarily constitute prosperity, mental peace and happiness, in the same way, the lack of material wealth does not necessarily constitute adversity, mental agitation or unhappiness.

A life of simplicity does not mean giving up all wealth and going to live off the land. It means living according to the necessities of life and not hoarding possessions as sources of happiness or due to some family obligation. It means not indulging in the egoism of jealousy by comparing oneself to others and trying to emulate their success or trying to look good in their eyes. The divine plan has prescribed a specific path for every individual. Therefore, you should live life according to the understanding that you have been given all of the necessary tools to accomplish the goals of your life. Therefore, while continuing to strive for better conditions in life the underlying understanding should be that if riches are to come it is by the will of the Divine. Likewise, if adversities come it is for the same reason. Both adversities and prosperities come to a person according to their karmic history as fruits of past actions. Therefore, in order to promote positive situations in the future, all you need to do is concentrate on correct actions in the present which are guided by the correct attitude and understanding.

Self-Publishing

What Is Self-Publishing?

In ancient times a few used stone and papyrus as the first publishing instruments. Today many can use the miracle of the computer. Self-Publishing is the act of producing a book yourself as opposed to writing a book and then approaching a someone else, like a major publishing house, in the hopes that they will like it and print it for you. When a writer writes a book, he or she has the choice of completing a manuscript and then paying a printer to print it in book form, or submitting it to a publishing house which will evaluate it. The publishing house may decide to pick up the title and either buy the rights to the book, accept it with the condition that some changes be made now, or that they have the right to make editorial changes or changes to the writing itself later. If they accept it and feel that it will be a popular title, they may offer a substantial advance on it. If it does well, they will continue to print and promote it to the mass market. They may also grant an advance on a sequel. The latter scenario is not the usual case however. Most often, books that do not offer a potential to sell to the mass market will not be accepted. Even if the book is accepted, there may be problems. If the book publisher orders 5,000 copies of the book and finds that it is selling slowly, they may discontinue its production and the book will go out of circulation when they sell out. The book will then become *Out Of Print*. The usual result of submissions of manuscripts to publishers is that most publishers will reject it.

Self-Publishing

Again, if it is accepted, chances are that the publisher will want to reserve the right to make changes or even rewrite certain portions of the manuscript.

    Self-Publishing means producing the book yourself. There are many degrees of production in which a Self-Publisher can engage. The benefits of Self-Publishing are manifold. First, you can have complete control over your work. You are the creator, writer and editor. While it is recommended that you create a manuscript and have others review it, it is you who are the final authority on what goes in or comes out of your literary creation. Secondly, you have the freedom to promote your book and keep your book in circulation as long as you like. Most importantly, you can have the versatility of making changes, revisions, additions, etc., at any time. This is not so easy when working with a publisher or when you are producing your books in large quantities. If you decide to Self-Publish, you face some daunting, but not insurmountable, obstacles. Perhaps the most important obstacle is ignorance. How do I go about publishing my own book? Where do I begin? The next frustrating problem is the finances. How much will it cost? This pamphlet will give a writer the basic steps involved in creating a book for less than a Commercial Book Printer would charge.

Self-Publishing
Working With Others to Produce Your Book

The method of producing a book, that will be presented in this manual goes beyond just writing or word-processing. It requires some knowledge of the computer and a few easy to learn programs. Many people also become intimidated when they peer into the tasks necessary to be a self-publisher. In the strict sense of the term self-publishing is when you do all the work from beginning to end. However, you should not take it upon yourself to produce a book and then print it yourself. You should attempt to take on as many of the design and composition (writing, editing, typesetting, composition and preparation of images, etc.) work though and when you have everything ready you can take it to the printer.

You should also consider another approach. If you are proficient at the writing but not so proficient at using the computer you should consider taking classes and learning as much as you can but you can also team up with someone who is well versed at the computer, ideally a family member or friend. For instance, if you purchase a computer for your teenager you will have an almost instant assistant to help you. They will learn a valuable skill for the future as they assist you in the present. In this manner, you will be able to move along quickly on the road to getting your book ready and develop closer relationships with your family and friends at the same time.

Self-Publishing

The Commercial Book Printer

A Commercial Book Printer will usually want you to print a minimum of 1,000 to 1,500 books at a time. This means that if you decide to publish on your own, through a Commercial Book Printer, you will have a house full of books unless you have access to a suitable storage space. This also means that you will need to invest a large chunk of your savings to produce that one book until you find enough bookstores and/or distributors to accept your books and pay you for them. A sample estimate from a Commercial Book Printer is included on the next page.

Self-Publishing

JEFFERSON Printing
QUOTATION

DATE: 10/16/97

Quotation #: 1354

Send to:
Cruzian Mystic Books
10260 SW 160th Terrace
Miami, FL 33157

E-MAIL:

TITLE OF BOOK: Book of My Life

(1) TRIM SIZE: 8.5 x 11　　　　　　　　　　TEXT BLEEDS: no
(2) NUMBER OF PAGES: 240　　　　　　　　TEXT SHEETFED: yes　WEB: (10)
(3) TEXT PRINTS: 1/c black
(4) TEXT STOCK: 50# white offset
(5) COVER PRINTS: 4-0-0-4 color process　　BINDING: perfect bound
(6) COVER STOCK: 10 pt. CIS　　　　　　　COVER COATING: UV (7)
　　SHRINK WRAP: in two's　　　　　　　　BULK PACK: yes
(8) TEXT FURNISHED: disk
(9) COVER FURNISHED: disk

HALFTONES: no

PRINTER TO FURN: complete proofs and cover
PUBL TO FURN:

　　　　　　　　　　　　　　　　　　　　Freight
(11) 1000　　　$3,694.00　　　　　　　　　$363.00
　　 1500　　　$4,479.00　　　　　　　　　$456.00

Self-Publishing

In the sample quotation on page 51, from a Commercial Book Printer, you can see the specifications of the quotation.

1-The proposed final (trim) book size will be 8½" X 11."
2-It will have 240 numbered pages.
3-The text will be of one color (1/c black).
4-The paper used for the interior of the book will be 50# white offset (standard).
5-The cover will be 4-0-0-4. This means that it will have four colors on one side, the outside (front and back cover), and no printing on the inside (inside front and inside back). Therefore, it is referred to as *four over zero.*

6-The paper stock that will be used for the cover is 10 point CIS. It is equivalent to 80# paper used by industrial copiers. This book will be a *Softcover* as opposed to a *Hardcover,* which is much more expensive to produce.

7-To protect the finish of the cover it will receive UV coating. This is also referred to as *film lamination.* 8-When you are advanced in the use of your computer, you can submit your work on disk. Otherwise, you can send it to the printer or copy service as a printed hard copy, i.e., 240 pages from your laser printer. If you submit it on disk you need to make sure that your file is compatible with the printer's computer system and program.

Self-Publishing

9-The cover can be submitted on disk or as film separations. You can take your work to a graphics output firm who can prepare color separations for you. This is a good way to go because you can do this locally. Then you can see what the finished product will look like and make any necessary changes or corrections before sending it off.

10-Some printers use a WEB press. This means that they take your pages and photograph them in order to produce negatives that will be used to make plates. These plates will be used to print your book on the web sheets. This is the traditional printing method using a press. However, a growing number of printers are upgrading to all computerized output systems that do not require negatives. But these computerized systems are still not as cost effective as the older WEB systems. This means that the production costs are likely to be more, depending on where you go. So you can inquire at local printers to see what they can provide and at what cost.

Self-Publishing

11-Based on the quotation above, the cost per book will be $4.06 for 1000 books and $4.94 for 1500 books. See below.

    $3,694.00 Printing Cost
+ _____ 363.00 Freight from the printer to you.[1]
= $4,057.00

So the cost per book for 1000 books will be $4,057.00 / 1000 = $4.06

    $4,479.00 Printing Cost
+ _____ 456.00 Freight from the printer to you.[1]
= $4,935.00

The cost per book for 1500 books will be $4,935.00 / 1500 = $3.29.

Self-Publishing

Reprints will be a little less, $3,447 for 1000 books or $2.84 each plus freight, and $4,253.00 plus freight for 1500 books. The reprints will be less if you are going to reprint exactly the same pages and exactly the same cover. This is because the same negatives can be reused. However, if you want to make revisions or additions, etc., you will incur additional charges.

The other drawback to this system, as discussed before, is that you must invest a sizable amount of money that will be just sitting there, collecting dust, until you sell the books. It is not cost efficient to print less than 1000 books through this method because if you produce less than this amount, the cost per book will be very high in comparison to what you can sell it for. You will not have any room to make a profit to produce new books, pay for your time and effort or support yourself while you promote the book or work on new books.

How The Book Industry Works

The book industry works as follows. The ordinary method of selling books is through bookstores, but how do they get the books from the author or publisher such as yourself? First of all the manuscript for the book is written by someone, the author. The manuscript then goes to the publisher who will finance its production if it is accepted. After editing and proof-

Self-Publishing

ing, the publisher will the send the manuscript to the Book Printer who will make it into book form, and then work to get the distributors to offer the book as part of their catalog. The publisher will promote the book, trying to interest bookstores in carrying it so that customers can see it. The author needs to make special appearances at bookstores to speak about the books and sign autographed copies. If the author conducts seminars, these sessions can be recorded and advertised within the book as well. Seminars, talks and book signings are necessary to get the word out about your book and its importance to the reader.

The Process of Getting a Book Made

(H)- Customer

(G)- Bookstores
↑

(F)- Distributor or Wholesaler or direct to bookstores
↑

E- Finished book
↑

(D)-Book Printer Method Ù (D-1) Or Copy Service Method
↑

Editing - Typesetting - Proofreading
↑

Send to Publisher or Self-Publish yourself
↑

(B)-(C)- Prepare and print your manuscript for printing or copying.
↑

(A)-Author

Self-Publishing

The Process of Getting a Book Made (Flow-chart)

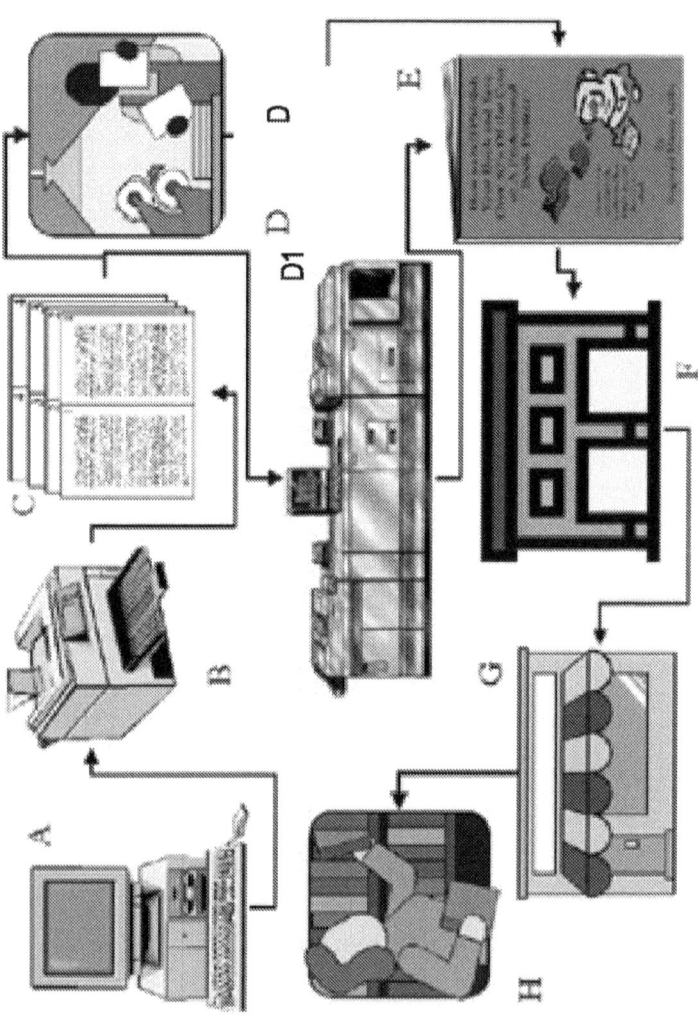

Most of the books that are sold can change many hands before they reach the customer, the reader. The flow chart on page 58 gives you an indication of the process.

The flowchart given above is the traditional route to getting a book published. It is important to understand that the publisher, distributors and bookstores do not provide their services for free. They charge a commission for their part in the process. Let's say that you want to produce this book. Each book will cost you $4.06. So what should the sales price be in order for you to make an adequate profit in order to continue printing more books? The question is what should the *retail price* be? How much will the customer need to pay at the bookstore?

Bookstores charge a commission of 40% to sell your book. Distributors charge a commission of 15%. If you want the traditional route, the publisher will want his or her cut for producing and financing the book as well. The distributor works as follows. The distributor takes your book on consignment at a 55% discount off the retail price. For example, if the retail price is $18.95, the equation will work as follows: $18.95 retail less $10.42 (55%) = $8.53 (45%) paid to you. Then they will sell it to bookstores at 40% of the retail or cover price[2] ($11.37). The bookstore will then sell it to the customer at the full cover price ($18.95) and take the profit of the sale, $18.95-$1 1.37 = $7.58 (40%).

Self-Publishing

After the costs you incurred to actually make the book, what do you get? If you publish through a traditional publishing company and the book is a good seller, you may get a percentage of the sales which may add up to a sizable amount. If the sales are slow you may get little or nothing at all. Therefore, the book needs to be well written, well put together, well promoted and well priced in order to turn a profit. However, if you publish the book yourself, you take in whatever monies come in when a book is sold, be it one book or a million. Then your costs of production become very important because they will determine whether or not there is any profit from the sales.

HOW TO PRICE YOUR BOOK

Some publishers give a formula for pricing a book. One example is to multiply the cost of your book by 8 (8X). However, this may not work sometimes, especially when considering short runs, because the cost structure is different. Also, the price depends on what the customer is willing to pay. Professionals may pay more than $50 for a book in their field. If selling to teenagers, the price will need to be low (less than $10). A business book may sell for $30. Generally, you should try to keep your price less than $20 in order to be accessible to the general market.

The 8X formula may work when you are printing 1,500 or more books at Book Printer prices, but short

Self-Publishing

runs need to be considered differently because the cost per book is higher. If you were to mark it up 8X the book would most likely be priced out of the market. Therefore, I recommend a markup multiplier of 3.5X for 8½" X 11" sized books and 5X for 5½" X 8½" sized books. Once you get the multiplier price, round it up to the nearest .95 price. For example, if you get a price of $14.40, round it up to $14.95. Then go to your local bookstores and check the section that has books that are similar to your proposed book and look at their covers, number of pages and most importantly, their prices. Then decide if your price is competitive with other books of the same size and subject or if you will need to make any adjustments. Your subject area may be in demand and the books in that area may be selling for $15.95. If so, raise your price to $15.95. The price of the book must appear on the back cover of the book on the lower or upper right hand side.

So, if your book will cost $4.06 each to produce, you need to take into account what the customer will pay and what you will have to pay to get the book into the customer's hands (printing costs, distribution, etc.). Therefore, if you think the book will sell for $18.95, because you have seen similar books in bookstores at this price, plug the cost figure into the formula and see if you will make a profit if you do it on your own. Ex. $4.06 X 8 = $32.48. This sales price is too high for the market so the 8X formula will not work here. Ex. $4.06 X 5 = $20.30. This price is closer to the market. Now you need to see if you can have any profit if you reduce the price to $18.95 in order to match the other books.

Self-Publishing

When you Self-Publish you bypass the publisher and go directly to the Book Printer or Copy Service yourself and avoid the publisher commission. You can work directly with book distributors. You contact them and send a review copy and they will let you know if they want to carry it. You can also work directly with the bookstores to avoid the higher distributor discount fee of 55%. While virtually all bookstores will pay the shipping fee, only a few distributors will foot the bill for the shipping. This will usually be part of your cost of doing business with the distributors. In addition to this, some distributors will ask for larger discounts, as high as 60% for larger quantity purchases. You can negotiate with them and give special pricing for large purchases such as hundreds or thousands of books at a time. If you are getting orders for 250-350 books at a time or more, you should have the books printed by a traditional book printer.

Keep in mind that bookstores prefer to deal with distributors because it is easier for them to order from one source instead of calling many publishers. It is also easier to return books to one place if necessary. However, if you have several books in your catalog, they will be more inclined to deal with you directly. If they do, you may want to extend special pricing to them. You can offer an additional discount such as 45% instead of the usual 40%, or you may offer them free freight. Remember that if you deal with bookstores directly, you are getting more profit from the

Self-Publishing

sale. So offering free freight or higher discounts may still be worthwhile since you mave to pay the freight to send the books to the distributor with an even higher discount rate. Look over your finances and see if you can afford to give any promotional offers. The bookstores will appreciate them and buy more of your books. In addition to this, you can start your own mailing list and catalog to send directly to customers. You should put a notice in the back of your book telling your customers that you have other publications in which they may have an interest. You should also include an order form at the end of your book (see the last page). Then they can contact you and order from you directly, and you can start a mailing list. You can sell them other books, your audio lectures, offer consulting services, etc., directly and bypass the book industry altogether. This allows you to keep the entire sale for yourself and not pay any commissions to anyone. This is the most profitable scenario for you although it takes some time to develop.

See the following chart which compares the potential profit when selling your books through the different avenues (Distributors, Bookstores, and Direct to customers) after having your book printed by a Book Printer. Keep in mind that with bookstore sales and direct sales to customers you do not pay the freight cost, they do.

Self-Publishing

Sales Projections Using the Book Printer Method

	Sales to book distributors	Sales to bookstores	Sales to customers direct
Sales Price	$18.95	$18.95	$18.95
Discount	-10.42	-7.58	0
Cost to print the book	-4.06	-4.06	-4.06

So you can see from the figures above, if you publish the book yourself and sell enough copies of it through all three routes (Distributors, Bookstores, and Direct to customers) you can make a sufficient profit to sustain your book publishing activities. Keep in mind that if it is possible for you to have 1,500 or more books printed by the Book Printer, the profit margin is greatly improved because the cost per book will be substantially lower than the Copy Method. However, if your sales are not proceeding fast enough, you will have a lot of money invested (in producing 1,500 books) and it will take a long time for you to get it back out. If you have other book ideas they will have to wait due to lack of funds.

Self-Publishing **Self-Publishing: The Copy Method®**

The solution to the latter problem is Self-Publishing using the system outlined in this volume, *The Copy Method®*. After years of trial and error I have discovered that it is not necessary to go through a traditional Commercial Book Printer to produce a book. What is necessary is that the author or Self-Publisher needs to do the work of first understanding the process of publishing, and then directing the production, and whenever possible, doing as much of the development and production work as he or she can. You may contact businesses in your area and find out if they can do the following work at the prices given or you can contact C.M Books for the companies that we use for our book production.

The big advantage of working this way is that you do not have to produce 1,000 or 1,500 books at a time and incur the big expense. You can produce as little as 100 books and reorder as your sales pick up. This will free up your cash to produce more books of the same title or of different titles. The advantage of producing other book titles if you have other great ideas is that even if your sales are slow for each book, you can sell more total books because you have more product choices for the bookstores and book readers to see. Instead of selling 50 of one book each month ($3.21 X 50 = $160.50 total profit per month), you can sell 250 if you have 5 books ($3.21 X 250 = $802.50 total

Self-Publishing
profit per month) or 500 if you have 10

books ($3.21 X 500 = $1,605.00 total profit per month), etc. Although, the quantity of sales per book may be low for each particular book, when put together they add up to a substantial amount. In the beginning you will need to reinvest some of the profits so that you can produce more books and promote your books.

1- You need to be able to put the cover of your book together yourself or contract someone who can create it as per your direction. Usually graphic arts companies that produce color separations, composites, computer output, etc., will have people in their staff who can do this work. Also you can contact the PMA^3 group which has many listings of people who specialize in producing book covers.

2- You will need to work with a copy service that you can give your manuscript to as a hard copy or on disk. I suggest that you search for a volume Commercial Copy Service that employs the latest technology. The state of the art industrial copiers are so good now that they rival the traditional Book Printer's quality. It is best if you find a company that can do the copies of the interior of the book and the binding as well. Even better, if you can find a company that can print out your covers, the body of the book as well as do the binding, you will have the best situation because you will not have to coordinate between different companies to get the work done.

Self-Publishing

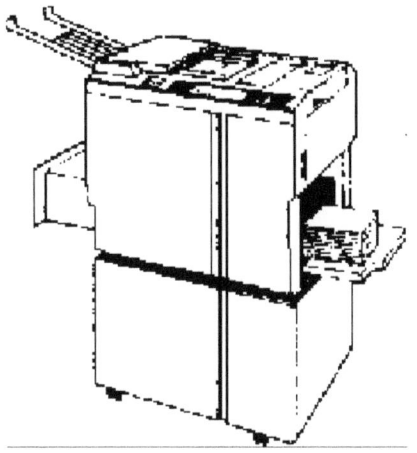

Above: An example of a low volume copy service copier.

Self-Publishing

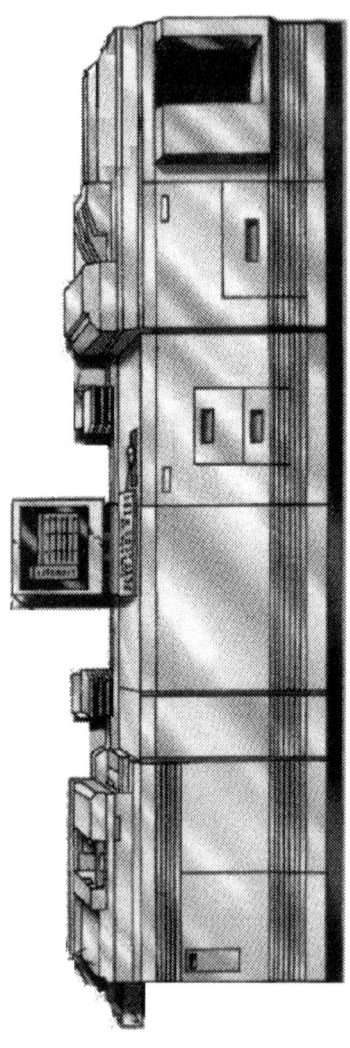

Above: An example of a high volume copier used at a Commercial Copy Service Company

Self-Publishing

3- The company that we use for the printing also does the binding. Also, if you can find such a company in your hometown, you will be able to avoid the freight charges. When meeting with them, you can show them the prices we are presenting in this booklet. If they cannot match the prices, you can also ask them to match the prices plus the freight charge that it would cost you to deal with an out of town Copy Service. If they can match that price it will still be a good deal for you because you will be able to work directly with someone in the area and avoid the freight time that it would take to send and receive your books. If you have to use an out of town service, you can alleviate the problem by asking them if they will drop ship a portion of the books directly to the bookstores or distributors. This way you can avoid the added cost and work of freight to you, and then your repackaging the books and sending them out to the bookstores and distributors. Be sure to examine samples of their work. On your first order, run as few as possible to see the quality and discuss what will be done with damaged or substandard copies before they begin to do the work. Do not accept anything that cannot be sold in Barnes and Noble or other major book store chains.

4- Once you have the companies lined up you can turn your work over to them. Then you must work on getting notices and press releases to the distributors and bookstores.

Self-Publishing

5- The following figures represent the costs of production that you should expect to incur if you use the Copy Method to produce your books. You should not expect an ordinary consumer copier center to give you the following prices. Copy companies such as Kinko's or Office Depot-Images, PIP Printing, Sir Speedy, etc., are usually geared towards the consumer market and not the commercial market. Try to locate a Commercial Copy Service that can meet the following prices or contact us for the name and address of the Commercial Copy Service we currently use.

6- <u>COVER:</u> If your copy service cannot print the cover, you will need to go to a commercial printing company to have them done separately. Then you can take them to the Commercial Copy Service for the binding of your book. Again, try to locate a Commercial Copy Service in your area that can meet the following prices, or contact us for the name and address of the Commercial Copy Service we use. You may need to order a minimum of 1,000 covers. They should cost no more than 55¢ for an 18"w X 11½" (8½" X 11" final size) cover and 45¢ for a 12.5" X 9" (5½" X 8½" final size) cover, plus freight charges of 12%. The price should include UV Coating. **DO NOT WASTE YOUR MONEY WITH VARNISH OR OTHER COVERINGS OTHER THAN UV.** Do not put your book in the marketplace without the UV coating.

Self-Publishing

Book covers without UV get damaged easily and you will get them returned by bookstores and customers. They will not want to deal with you, thinking that you are pushing a product that is below standard. The UV Coating provides a glossy protective covering which your book will need as it is handled from the printer to you, and finally to the reader. Also, it gives it a quality look. Once the book is completed you can have it sent to you via UPS, but if you are shipping 200 pounds or more you should use a freight company.[4] Choose a freight company that will send them on pallets all together so that they will not be separated, thrown or jostled, as an ordinary package carrier will do.

SHRINK WRAP

For added protection you can and should have the books shrink wrapped after they are put together and bound. The handling will be rough from the time they are made to the time they reach you and then during the freighting to the final buyers (distributors, customers or distributors. This will save you from receiving damaged copies which cannot be sold for full price so **have your books shrink wrapped!** This will cost you anywhere from 10¢ to 30¢ each depending on who does it for you **but its worth it!.**

The Cost of a 240 Page Book Produced with the Copy Method

8½" X 11" Book	Retail Price	# of pages	Copy Charge	Cover	Cutting	Binding	Freight	Total Cost Each
			8.5 X 11					
			1.35¢ per page					
Book of My Life	$18.95	240	$3.24	$0.55	$0.10	$0.75	$0.68	$5.32

Self-Publishing

Self-Publishing The

Cost For An 8½" X 11" Book

Thus, through the Copy Method you can produce the same 8½" X 11" book for $5.32 each, as opposed to $4.06 through the Book Printer, a difference of $1.26. The profit to you would look as follows.

$18.95	Sales Price
-	40% Bookstores
7.	15% Distributor or Wholesaler
58	Copy Method
-	Net profit to you. This is a 60% return
2.	
	your investment of $5.32.

Note that your total investment through the copy method is $532.04 to produce 100 books.

The total investment through the Book Printer Method is $4,057.00 to produce 100 because you must order 1000 books.[5]

This means that for the same investment amount that it takes to produce one book title through the Commercial Book Printer Method you could have produced 7+ different books ($4,057.00 / $532.04 = 7.63) through the Copy Service Method. Seven books available for sale means that you have more titles in your portfolio that you can show to bookstores and customers, and consequently more titles to sell. The profit is less per book, but because you can sell more books, you make up for the difference. What good is it if you can make more profit per book, but the large run of books sit in a closet in your home or in a warehouse and take a long time to sell, and at the same time ties up your money? The printing of 500 books or less is referred to as a *short run*. By producing more titles as short runs you can do more business and make more profit.

See the following chart which compares the potential profit when selling your books through the different avenues (Distributors, Bookstores, and Direct to customers) after having your book printed by the Copy Method. Keep in mind that in bookstore sales and direct sales to customers you do not pay the freight cost, they do.

Self-Publishing

Sales Projections Using the Copy Method

	Sales to book distributors	Sales to bookstores	Sales to customers direc
Sales Price	$18.95	$18.95	$18.95
Discount	-10.42	-7.58	0
Cost to print the book	-5.32	-5.32	-5.32
Net profit to you per book	$3.21	$6.05	$13.63

Self-Publishing

Galley Copies VS. Short Runs

Sometimes you may want to submit your manuscript to reviewers, publishers and distributors to get feedback from them on the desirability of the book and to get positive recommendations in the form of good reviews which you can advertise along with the book promotions you will do. The industry refers to the bound copies of the manuscript you will send out prior to publication as *Galley Copies*. Galleys may be tape or spiral bound, but even these formats will be costly. You will want to present your best looking product always, and as we discussed, a Commercial Book Printer will charge astronomical prices to do less than 500 books on a short run. The shorter the run to be printed the higher the price per book will be. Some advertise more reasonable rates (Ex. $380.00 for 100 copies of a 96 page *perfect bound*† 5½" X 8½" size book with a two color cover = $3.80 per book.). The cost is still much higher than the Copy Method and you get a four-color cover with the Copy Method, not just two! See the calculation below. Also, Commercial Book Printers do not like to work on short runs. The price for short runs at a regular Commercial Book Printer can range from $8 to $11 or more for each copy, depending on the size of the book. If you are selling less than 350 books of a single title per month it is more cost effective to use the Copy Production Method instead of the Book Printer Method to produce your galley copies.[6] The Copy Method is more

Self-Publishing

cost effective even for producing your Galleys when you compare the Galley prints through the Copy Method versus the Galley prints from the Commercial Book Printer. †(will be discussed later)

$3.80 for short runs from the Commercial Book Printer with two-color cover.
- $2.05 for short runs through the Copy Method with four-color cover.
=$1.76 total savings per book! This is means a savings of 46% that you can use to print more books to send to more people or to sell to bookstores.

Don't forget that the $3.80 for short runs from the Commercial Book Printer only includes two colors on the cover. So the price would be much higher if the Commercial Book Printer tried to match the Copy Method by doing the job with four colors. The Commercial Printer gave me a quote of $760.00 for 100 copies of a 96 page, perfect bound 5½" X 8½" size book with a four color cover = $7.60 per book! So your savings are higher than 50% and you get the same or better product for less. You can produce twice as many books through the Copy Method! See below.

Cost of a 100 Page Book Produced With the

Title	Retail Price	# of pages	Cost/page 5.5 X 8.5 .675¢ per page	Cover	Cutting	Binding	Freight	Total Cost Each
5½" X 8½" Book		100	$0.68	$0.45	$0.10	$0.75	$0.07	$2.05

Self-Publishing

The Cost For a 5½" X 8½" Book Through the Copy Method

The cost per book goes down when you are producing a 5½" X 8½" sized book because of the smaller format. A special formatting technique will allow you to use half of the 8½" X 11" sheet and thereby cut the cost of the copies in half. Also, the cover will be smaller and will therefore cost less. The weight will be less, and will therefore cost less. The retail prices for 5½" X 8½" sized books range from $8.95 or less to $18.95, depending on the amount of pages and the other factors described above related to demand, who you are writing for and interest in the book. We will work with a price of $15.99 for a book containing 264 pages. The costs break down is as follows if you sell your book through distributors and bookstores. Also see the chart on the following page.

$15.99	Sale Price
− 6.39	40% Bookstores
− 2.39	15% Distributor or Wholesaler
− 3.27	Copy Method
=$ 3.94	Net profit to you.

Note that your total investment through the Copy Method is: $327.00 to produce 100 books.

Note that your total investment through the Book Printer Method is: $760.00 to produce 100 books. This is a big difference.

Self-Publishing

Cost of a 264 Page Book Produced With the Copy Method

Title	Retail Price	# of pages	Cost/page	Cover	Cutting	Binding	Freight	Total Cost Each
			5.5 X 8.5					
			.675¢ per page					
5½" X 8½" Book	$15.95	264	$1.78	$0.45	$0.10	$0.75	$0.20	$3.28

Self-Publishing
The Idea For The Subject of Your Book

(16) "I have not been an eavesdropper or pried into matters to make mischief." <u>Variant: I have not spied.</u>*
>Do not enter the house of anyone,
>Until he admits you and greets you;
>Do not snoop around in his house; let your eye observe in silence.
>Do not speak of him to another outside,
>Who was not with you;
>A great deadly crime this is.†
>*Ancient Egyptian Book of Coming Forth By Day †Ancient Egyptian Sage Ani*

If you decide to proceed with your book project, you will need to consider what you would like the subject of your book to be unless you already have a manuscript written. The first thing you need is an idea and as discussed earlier, it should be in line with righteousness and truth. In recent years, the emergence of scandal tabloids in print and on television, romance novels, pornography, violence and other similar publications fostering mental unrest in peoples minds in order to excite them to buy a product offer good examples of unrighteous publishing, based on greed. They are a symptom of mental weakness in society and the cure for this problem is righteous publishing. The publication of ideas and subjects that uplift the mind, bring people hope and enlightenment. Tantalizing scandal tell-all books and newspapers bring short-term prosperity to the publisher but in the long run they damage everyone's ability to discover true mental peace. What is the book going to be about and what is its purpose? Then you need to know the audience for which you are writing and how best to reach them. Your idea may only affect a certain group of people. It may be very specific. If it is, Self-Publishing is definitely the way for you to go because your audience may be too small to generate the kind of sales to interest a major book publisher. Also, your sales may be slow due to the small population you are reaching. If you later find out that the idea is hot, after you published the book yourself, you can still negotiate with the major book publishers, who will now be eager to take on your book, or you can go to the Book Printer yourself and place larger print run orders.

In any case, you should feel passionate about the idea. Your concerns should not be about the popularity of the idea, but how well the idea comes across to the reader. If you need to, you should take a writing course. You should edit and re-edit your book yourself, as well as having at least one other person edit it. Then you can allow others such as trusted colleagues, family members, friends and even professional book reviewers to look over your manuscript. Finally, once your manuscript is typeset, composed and ready to be given to the printer, it needs to be proofread. The proofreader should check the spelling, typesetting, layout, etc.

Sometimes people become overly concerned with the idea for the book and focus on making money or trying to produce something sensational, intriguing, scandalous, controversial, etc. If you are thinking about what is going to make you rich, you will probably miss

Self-Publishing

the mark. Also, greediness in any area of life ultimately tends to bring disappointments and frustrations in the end. Writing should be treated as an art, and in order for the artistic inspiration to flow, your heart needs to be contemplating the higher goals of the writing project. You need to ask yourself questions like, what is it within me that is trying to come out through my writing? How can my ideas help others and how can it be explained in terms that they can understand? When you bring forth something artistic by means of virtuous intentions, you are conveying something that is really worthwhile. People ultimately want truth and reality, and not sensationalism and artificial controversy. Ultimately they will see through that which is faddish and dishonest, and the book will have a limited appeal and a limited life span. If you are honest and sincere your book will have a greater chance of staying in demand for a long time.

It is legitimate to have concerns about the commercial appeal of your work, but this should not be the overriding factor. If this is your main concern, your work will not have substantive value and the consequence is that it may sell as a fad item, but will probably not have staying power in the marketplace. It will be a fake, and it will not help anyone. The money you derive from it will not serve you either. It will be fast in coming and fast in leaving you as well. Seek what is real in your life, and then seek to write about the reality that you feel inside. This will connect with people always, because it will touch what is real in them and not what is faddish and transient in human emotions, feelings and thoughts. When you feel comfortable with the idea you will then be ready to proceed with the book production process.

What You Will Need To Do The Work

Above: A Typical Computer Setup

If you decide to design your own book and cover there are some tools you will need. If you want to produce the manuscript alone, you will need a computer, a laser printer and a Desktop-publishing program which you will use with the computer. If you want to produce the manuscript as well as the cover

Self-Publishing

you will need a graphics program, a scanner and a color printer in addition to the computer and the Desktop-publishing program.

1. COMPUTER: You will need a computer with the following minimum specifications: 133-Megahertz (speed) or higher, 32 Megabytes of ram memory, 1.5 Gigabytes of hard disk space, a 16X CD-ROM (Total cost of computer IBM compatible $700).[7]

2. MONITOR: You will need a 17-inch monitor ($300-$400). If you are working only with text (manuscript), a 14" or 15" monitor will do fine. However, if you are working with a lot of graphics you will want to have nothing less than a 17" monitor.

3. WORD PROCESSING PROGRAM- The word processing program can be used for books which will contain a minimum of graphics or many simple graphics and text. Examples of top of the line word processing programs are *Microsoft Word®* and *Word Perfect®*. Word is excellent for producing basic 8½" X 11" sized books because it affords advanced word processing features such as table of contents, index and grammar check, along with the added advantage of being able to add footnotes. You can import preexisting graphics into it in order to spruce up the look and feel of the pages and enhance the understanding of the subject. You can use Microsoft Word for the 5½" X 8½" sized books

but you will have to reposition the footnotes manually. Also, other features will be harder to use. Therefore, the Desktop-publishing programs are better suited for the smaller format books. This book was written in Microsoft Word® and composed in Pagemaker®. The custom graphics were produced with Adobe PhotoShop®. The cover was produced with Microsoft Publisher®. Also, many of the graphics used are free graphics provided with the Microsoft Publisher program. With Microsoft Word you can place and manipulate graphics fairly freely. However, the desktop-publishing programs offer the widest latitude for placing graphics and working with text-blocks.

4. <u>DESKTOP PUBLISHING PROGRAM-</u> The desktop publishing program can be used for text which will incorporate extensive graphics and text. Examples of advanced desktop-publishing programs are *PageMaker®, Microsoft Publisher®* and *Quark Express®*. They can easily generate a table of contents and an index. They are adequate for producing your book if you do not intend to add footnotes. A program such as Microsoft Publisher is easier to learn and is adequate for producing your book if you do not intend to add an index or footnotes. It offers some of the features of a Word Processor like Microsoft Word, and some of the features of an advanced publishing program such as PageMaker. However, it lacks many important

Self-Publishing

features which the advanced Self-Publisher will want, such as the ability to index, automatically assign table of contents entries, link graphics and be able to view them while liked (enabling you to work with a smaller and easier to handle file) and other features. Cutting and pasting by hand is a stone-age way to work. With these programs you can perform these tasks in a flash. This is espessially useful for teachers. As stated earlier, the desktop-publishing programs offer the widest lattitude for placing graphics and working with text-blocks. You can more easily manipulate various articles and combine them with clip-art. Clip-art are images, provided either with the desktop-publishing program or sold separately, which can be placed in your publication or manuscript to enhance the look and feel of your presentation. This book contains several clip-art images as well as images which were prepared exclusively for this book. These programs are better suited for producing the 5½" X 8½" sized books because it is easier to format the pages in their environment. You can obtain *templates* for the 8½" X 11" sized books and 5½" X 8½" sized books for use in the PageMaker or Publisher pro-grams from C.M. Books (305) 378-6253. These will save you the formatting time, so you can immediately get started writing your project.

    5. <u>Graphics program-</u> Computers and graphics programs seem intimidating, but once you get started,

Self-Publishing

especially with the correct guidance, you will discover that the problem is 99% fear of the computer. You should bring all of your images into the computer, manipulate them there, and then place them into your publication. It is not as hard as it sounds once you get into it. You may also want to take some classes at your local computer store or adult education program, or work with someone who is familiar with the programs. If you will be doing a lot of work with your own images you will need a good graphics program. *PhotoShop*® is ideal for this purpose. Once you create the images for your cover you can put everything together in PageMaker, Word or Publisher. When producing your cover you can create it completely in PhotoShop or you can create the pictures in PhotoShop and then put the cover together in one of the desktop-publishing programs, *PageMaker*®, *Quark Express*® or *Illustrator*®. Quark and Illustrator are good because they not only allow you to place your images in the positions you desire but you can create clean, sharp text on your cover design.[8]

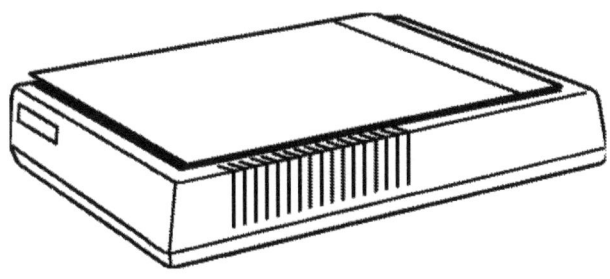

Above: Flatbed Scanner

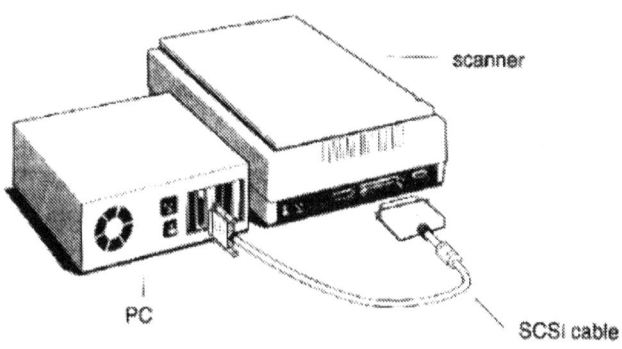

6. <u>FLATBED SCANNER:</u> Peripheral equipment should include a flatbed scanner ($100-$200). It may be connected to the computer in several different ways. You should check with your computer supplier for the latest information since technology in this field is changing almost monthly.

Self-Publishing

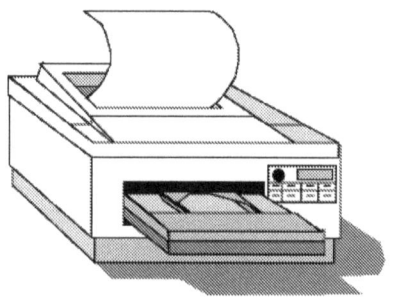

Above: The Laser Printer

7.   LASER PRINTER: You will use a laser printer to print proofs of your literary work as well as the final manuscript which will be sent to the printer.(Cost $$200-$250)

Above: The Inkjet Printer

8.   The inkjet printer: The ink-jet printer will be used to produce working copies and proofs of your covers. The technology has advanced so far that a rela-

Self-Publishing

tively inexpensive inkjet printer will produce virtually the same image you will see as the final product. We recommend the Epson Stylus Color II or IIs Inkjet Printer. (Cost approximately $1 00-250)

If you decide to do the work yourself begin with the basic computer hardware outlined above along with trhe following programs.

1- Microsoft Publisher
2- Adobe Photoshop

What A Book Printer And Outside Professionals Can Do For You

A Professional Book Printer will usually take your manuscript and your cover artwork when it is ready for printing. The interior of your book will need to be properly typeset and ready for printing. Generally, you will need to have everything ready for them. They will not accept the job unless they have a publishing staff available to do the work for you. This may cost you anywhere from $45-$ 100 per hour of their time for working on your cover alone. Typesetting costs can run $6-$7 per page for a 6 X 9 sized book, and $10 per page for an 8½ X 11 size. With some diligence and hard work you can learn to typeset your own book. The task is made easier with the Microsoft Word and

Self-Publishing

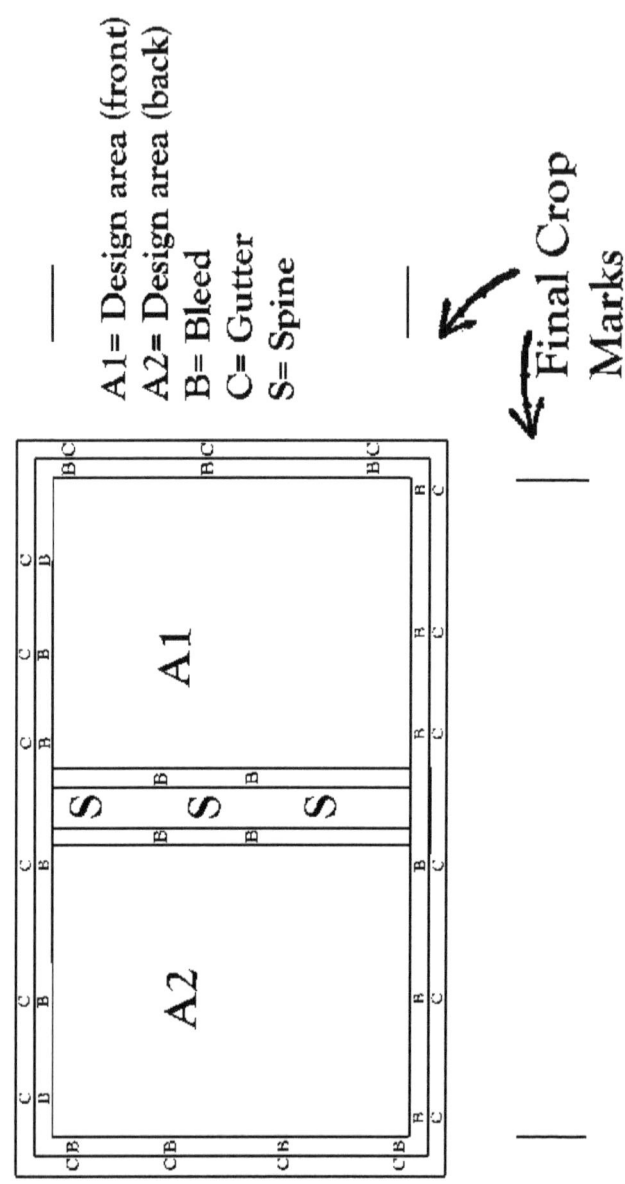

96

Self-Publishing

Adobe PageMaker programs. A copy editor may charge $15 per hour and a proofreader $15 per hour.

The Inside Text And Artwork

The printing process involves the use of paper and colors. There are two main components of a book. The first is the inside of the book and the second is the cover itself. Production of books that have color on the inside along with the text is extremely expensive and should not be attempted by the beginning Self-Publisher on a limited budget. You should be satisfied with black ink on white 20 pound paper for the interior portion of your book. If you have any pictures in your book, you can prepare them as gray-scale images with 85 lines per inch (lpi) resolution. You will want to use line art as well. This is the easiest format to work with and to print using the laser printer. The gray-scale images may require some special adjustments when you are about to print them out, depending on the printer you use. Images are recommended because they provide a greater visual impact for the subject of the book. They engage the reader in a way that the text cannot (one picture is worth a thousand words). Your efforts in giving color to your production should be reserved for the cover of the book.

Self-Publishing

Producing The Cover For Your Book

First you need to know what size your book will be when it is finished. For the purpose of this manual we will work with two sizes, 5½" (W) X 8½" (H) and 8½" (W) X 11" (H). The cover can be produced in one of three ways.

1-You can design it on a computer and format it for printing yourself using your own original artwork with the equipment and programs described above.

2-You can design it on a computer, using free (non-llicensed) artwork provided with many graphics programs and then let the company who will produce your cover finish formatting the job (for printing).

3-You can design it using your own artwork, then turn it over to a person who can scan it into the computer and format it for printing. If you contract a graphics firm to produce the cover for you, the cost may run from $500-$ 1,500 or more. If you need to purchase artwork or photos to use for the design which are not available for free use, the right to use them may cost from $500-800.

So you see, if you can do much of the work yourself you can save a great deal of money on the production of your book. This is particularly true if you produce several titles. The savings can be enormous,

Self-Publishing

as much as several thousands of dollars. If you decide to produce the artwork yourself on the computer, you probably will not have much difficulty in formatting the cover for the final printing with some simple instruction.

When producing the cover you will need to take care to work within the proper margins and leave enough area for bleeds (when color goes to the edge of the final trim size of the book). See the drawing on the next page.

The crop marks are the lines where the person doing the binding will cut the book once the cover and interior sheets of the book are bound. You should leave at least a ½" margin from the design area to the crop. Also, you should leave another ½" margin from the crop area to the outer edge (gutter) in order to have enough bleed area.

You will also need to leave area for the spine. A manuscript for an 8½" X 11" sized book containing 200 pages printed on one side only is in reality 100 sheets of paper when the typeset and composed originals are copied onto the sheets that will make up the book. This is because these sheets will be copied on the front and on the back. So you need to know how much spine area will be needed to accommodate 100 sheets of paper. See the list below for determining how much spine area to leave.

Cover Design Specifications

Spine
1/16"   1 to 15 sheets
1/8"   16 to 30 sheets
1/4"   31 to 60 sheets
3/8"   61 to 90 sheets
1/2"   91 to 120 sheets
5/8"   121 to 150 sheets
3/4"   151 to 180 sheets

So the specs for a 200-page 8½" X 11" sized book will be as follows:

Total working area =1 8½"w X 12"
Design area on front cover = 8" X 10"
Design area on back cover = 8" X 10"
Spine area ½"
Bleed Area ½"[9]
Gutter area ½"

---

[9] In order to be safe you can work with an additional ¼" of margin so that you will be sure to avoid any problems with the crop marks. This will decrease the design area to 8" X 9¾"

Self-Publishing

Self-Publishing

Colors On The Cover

How do people notice a book? The outer appearance and inside composition of your book are the keys to answering this question. When the cover has one color (black ink on white paper), it is referred to as a one-color cover. It can also have two or three colors. The less colors used, the less the cost of the cover will be. However, while there are many artistic ways in which one, two or three colors can be used, these will not provide the full impact of real life. For that you need to use a four-color process. It is only in this process which will allow you to have the full range of colors so that you can create virtually any design you want, including original pictures, paintings, etc. The cover is the first thing a person notices when they see your book. Therefore, you should not be frugal with the production and use of colors for the cover.

Above: The finished cover.

Self-Publishing

Self-Publishing **The Bar Code & ISBN Number**

Another important aspect of your book is the *Barcode*. The mass book industry is based on the barcode system. The barcode is a picture that contains a set of bars that contain mathematical information related to your book (ISBN number and the price of your book) . The barcode is not the same as an ISBN number although the ISBN number is used to generate the barcode. You need to obtain an ISBN number. The ISBN is the unique number which is assigned by the book industry to your book and which the industry uses to describe the book and to locate its publisher, you.

Above: Sample barcode.

The barcode is to be placed on the lower right hand corner of the back cover of the book. The major book distributors, such as Baker and Taylor, will not accept books that are not perfect bound and which do not include a barcode.

Above: Back cover of the book displaying the barcode.

The barcode can be created on your computer with the use of a program for producing barcodes. It is especially cost effective to buy the program if you will produce more than ten books. There are companies that produce barcodes for $15 to $25 dollars each. However, if you are going to have your cover produced from your artwork saved on disk, you can produce the barcode and also save it on disk. It can then be incorporated electronically with the cover composite when the time comes to print the covers. The program to produce the barcodes currently costs around $200.

The Setup For Copying 5½" X 8½" Format Books

In order to maximize your use of the 8½" X 11" sheet of paper you can use a technique called "two up typesetting setup." This means that you will have two sets of identical text on the same sheet, side by side, in a succession from the beginning with page 1 to the last page. See the following picture.

This is the basic setup for the interior portion of your book, and is one of the keys to making the Copy Method of book-making work. It is a simple process to set up. However, if you do not set it up correctly, the printout will not come out right on the page and the final product will be crooked or misaligned.

Self-Publishing

Self-Publishing

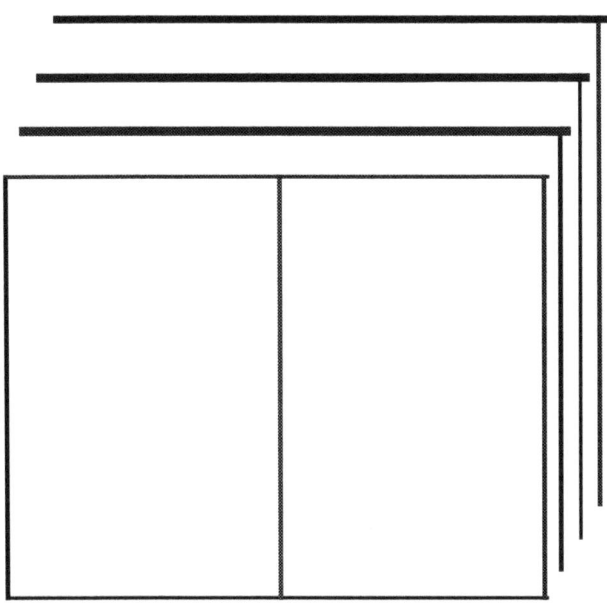

Above: The set up for printing a 5½" X 8½" sized book using 8½" X 11" sheets of paper.

When you print out your manuscript, you will actually be printing two sets of the same text on each sheet of 8½" X 11" paper. On either side of the sheet you will have the same text. This means that on sheet one you will have two texts of page one of your book. On sheet two you will have two texts for page two. On sheet three you will have two texts for page three, and so on.

Self-Publishing

When setting up your page, use a 1" or ½" margin from the outer edge of your text area to the edge of the paper. The area within the margins (grayed) will include all your text, graphics (clip-art, scanned in art or original art productions with the graphics program), headers and footers. The margin you will use depends on the desired layout that you want the book to have. How much space do you want to use?

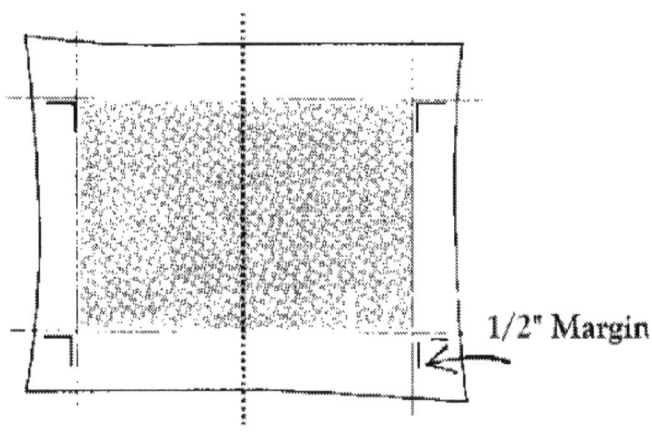

When you work with your computer program, your setup should look something like the following picture.

Note: This book was prepared in the PageMaker program.

Self-Publishing

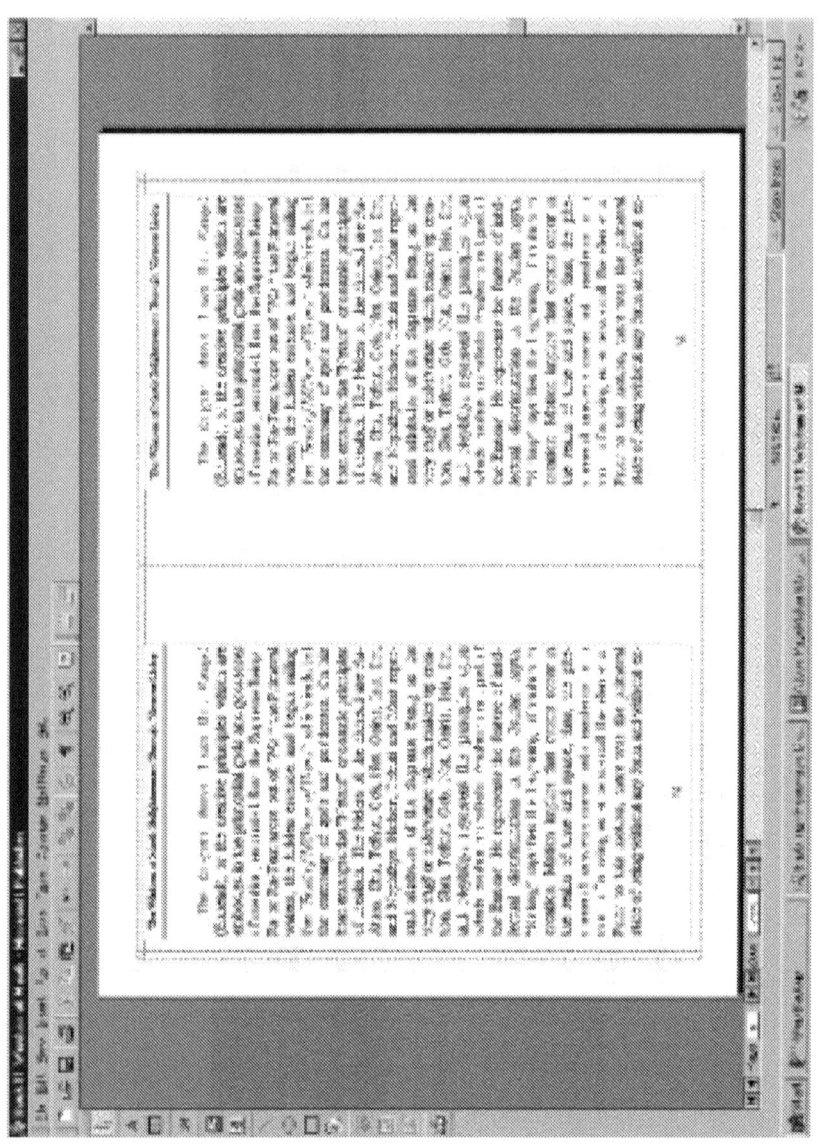

Above: A manuscript prepared in Microsoft Publisher. The screen shows one 8½" X 11" sheet with two identical text columns that will yield two 5½" X 8½" books.

Self-Publishing

The layout and composition of your pages are important, because these will carry forth your ideas. A good layout will employ text and graphics to bring the ideas to the reader both intellectually and visually.

You will want to use headlines, text, page numbers, and pictures. Once you have set up your text (composition and typesetting) you can proceed to print out your manuscript. See below.

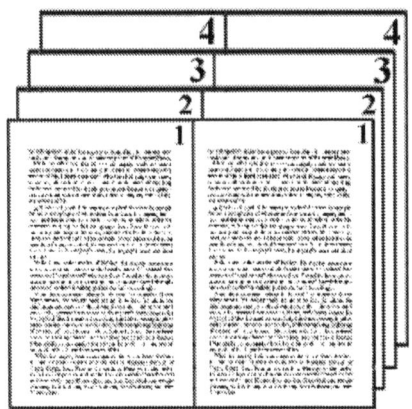

Above: Printed 8½" X 11" sheets with identical text on each side.

Self-Publishing

For the final product, the sheets will be copied on both sides. This means that page 2 will be behind page 1. Page 4 will be behind page 3, and so on. See below

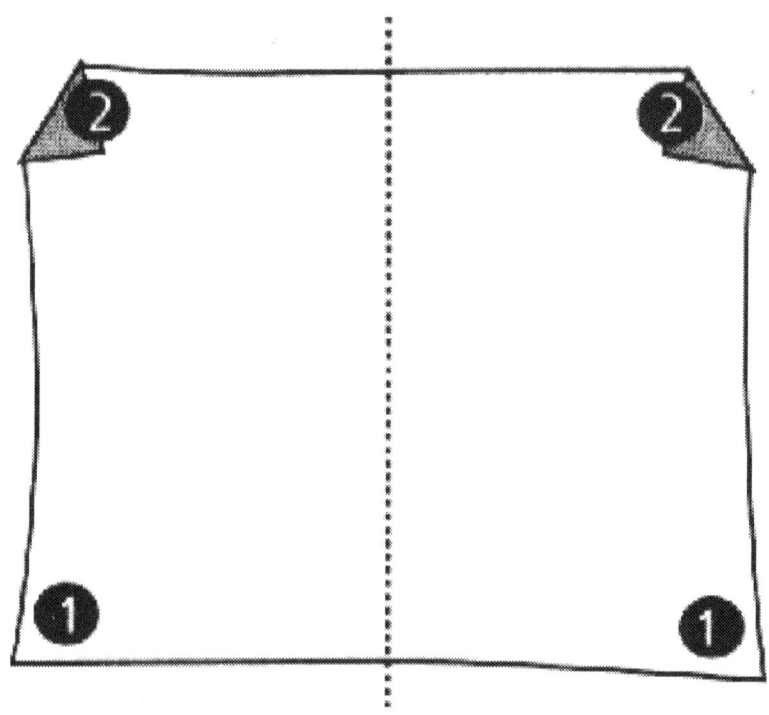

The next step in the process is the cutting. The Copy Service will run 100 sets (or as many as you order) of the book. Then they will cut the stack of 8½" X 11" sheets in half with an industrial cutter. This will yield two 5½" X 8½" unbound interior sections of your book. See Below.

Self-Publishing

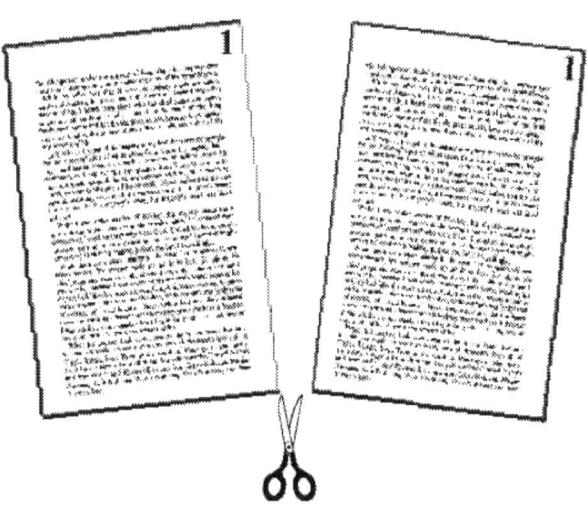

The next step in the process is the binding. The Copy-Binding Service will take the new 5½" X 8½" sections and bind them with the cover by placing special glue on the interior of the spine.

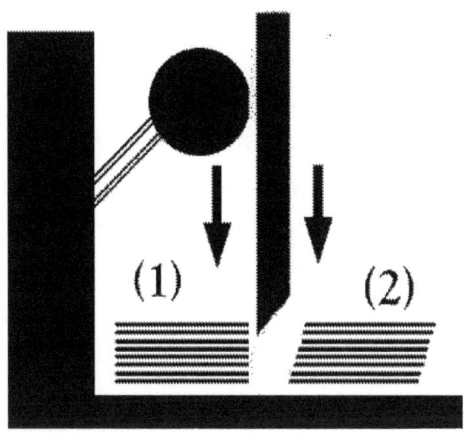

Self-Publishing

The clip-art image above is a representation of an industrial paper cutter. The 8½" X 11"sheets are placed on the base and then the cutter moves down and cuts the 8½" X 11"sheets into two identical sets, (1) and (2), of 5½ X 8½"stacks. These will be bound with the book cover.

The Cover And The Interior Of The Book

Many people do not realize the importance of the cover of a book. While it is true that you cannot always judge a book by its cover, you cannot easily sell a book that has an un-inviting cover. The mass market consumer is used to looking for materials that are slick, shiny and attention catching. Also, there is so much competition that the cover is the most important aspect of a book that most people will see at a glance. In this modern age of multimedia, video and color magazines, there are some minimum standards which any book needs to meet. These are listed below.

1- The book must have a color cover.
2- The book must be perfect bound.
3- The book should have at least 100 numbered pages.
4- The content of the cover should give an idea as to the subject of the book. It should invite the reader to open the book to find out more about the subject.

The flat edge at the left of the book is the perfect bound spine.

THE BINDING: There are several types of binding used for publications. Some of these are saddle stitch, spiral, coil, tape, and perfect. You should never produce your book in any format other than perfect binding unless it is a technical manual which people will want to lay flat easily. Examples of manuals are cook books, auto repair book and self publishing manuals. Perfect binding provides the professional look that the

Self-Publishing

distributors and bookstores want, and holds up better when used by the reader.

Selling Your Book

There are many places where you can sell your book. They fall under three major categories: Bookstores, Distributor Sales or Direct Sales. We discussed these earlier, but I want to re-emphasize the latter category, the direct sales to customers. You should collect the names of any person who may have shown an interest in your work, and send regular mailings to them, at least three times per year. Let them know what you are doing, where you are speaking, what new publications you are producing and what taped lectures they can obtain from you in reference to your books. You can develop a catalog of your products at a very low cost. For less than 50¢ you can create a 24-page catalog that will promote your books in a professional manner. You may obtain a catalog template from C.M. Books for use in the Microsoft Publisher or Adobe PageMaker Formats.

Self-Publishing

Above: Example of one of the 5½" X 8½" sized catalogs used by C.M. Books.

Many people do not realize that although being an author sounds glamorous and can open doors to great opportunities, there are very few authors who actually make a living by writing books. In order to have a livable income you need to offer more than just your

Self-Publishing

book. You need to offer seminars, lectures and sequels to your work. You need to make sure that your readers know that these items are available, and that you are available to answer questions about your works, etc. In short, this needs to be your life. There-fore, don't do it to make money, but do it to fulfill your inner need for expression as an artist and to give something beneficial to the world. Then you will not need to worry about money. Everything you need will come to you when you need it, even fame and fortune.

You can obtain a mailing list program that can output mailing labels for you. When you have over 200 names, you can begin using the Post Office Bulk Mail Service which will save you money on postage.

Self-Publishing

Consignment Sales

Many bookstores will request that you give them your books on consignment for 30 to 90 days. This means that you are actually giving them a loan in the form of the investment you have in your books. You are not a bank, so it is recommended that you stay out of any consignment arrangements with bookstores. Besides, very often you will encounter small businesses that may be doing well one month and then have cash flow problems the next. You may get a call telling you that the money is coming, but never receive it. You will eventually have to call a collection agency to try to get them to pay. Worse still, they may go out of business, leaving you without cash or books. The answer is simple. Establish a policy and stick to it ALWAYS, unless you do not mind putting your money at risk needlessly. You may feel that you can trust others at their word. You may even feel like giving someone a chance as you would have liked someone to give you a hand, but you must always realize that they may have unforseen problems which in the end will affect you adversely. If you sell by COD (Cash On Delivery), you should request payment in cash and not check. If you want to accept checks, you can use a check guaranteeing service such as Telecheck. COD sales should be limited if you have limited funds because the time in between when you send the book and receive the payment is time without cash. In addition, if the customer does not accept the COD, you are out the cost of the postage, an probably the materials will be returned to you in a damaged condition. If you have

Self-Publishing

many COD sales, your cash-flow may be too low to pay your expenses. The cash flow is the amount of cash available during a given period of time. When more money goes out and than what comes in, the cash flow will be low. This situation is sometimes referred to as a negative cash flow.

You should consider entering into consignment arrangements only with the major book distributors such as Baker and Taylor, New Leaf Distributing, Barnes and Noble, etc., and only if they request it. They are reliable companies with a strong position in the book business. However, it is recommended that you move slowly so as not to overextend yourself. Learn how to budget your funds. Make sure that you always have enough to produce the books you need to have on hand to be able to fill the orders you are receiving. Otherwise you will lose sales by not having the books in stock because you are waiting for payments from your consignment sales.

The major distributors like to work on a 90 day system. They will pay you for the books that have sold within 90 days of the day of the sale. You can see that this option may require you to keep a sum of money invested. So you need to move slowly and budget for the amount of books you need to send to them. Fill their order as soon as you can, but do not allow your cash flow to be negative because this situation will cause problems that will ripple over to the rest of your operations.

Self-Publishing

Templates

You can obtain Templates for the 8½" X 11" sized book layouts, 5½" X 8½" sized book layouts for use in the PageMaker or Publisher programs and Cover Layouts for use in the PhotoShop program from C.M. Books (305) 378-6253. These will save you the formatting time and you can immediately get started writing your project.

Templates for book page layouts*:

1- 8½" X 11" for Microsoft Word $20.00
2- 8½" X 11" for Microsoft Publisher $20.00
3- 8½" X 11" for Adobe PageMaker $20.00
4- 5½" X 8½" for Microsoft Word $20.00
5- 5½" X 8½"" for Microsoft Publisher $20.00
6- 5½" X 8½"" for Adobe PageMaker $20.00

Templates for Book Covers*:

1- 8½" X 11" for Adobe PhotoShop Cover $20.00
2- 5½" X 8½" for PhotoShop Cover $20.00

Template for Catalog*:

1- Catalog- 24 pages - 5½" X 8½" size
For use in Microsoft Publisher $50.00

All templates are supplied on 3 1/2" diskettes for IBM compatible computers

Self-Publishing

only. They may work on Apple computers but no guarantee is given.

Self-Publishing

Below: Example of a template for page layout using the Adobe PageMaker program.

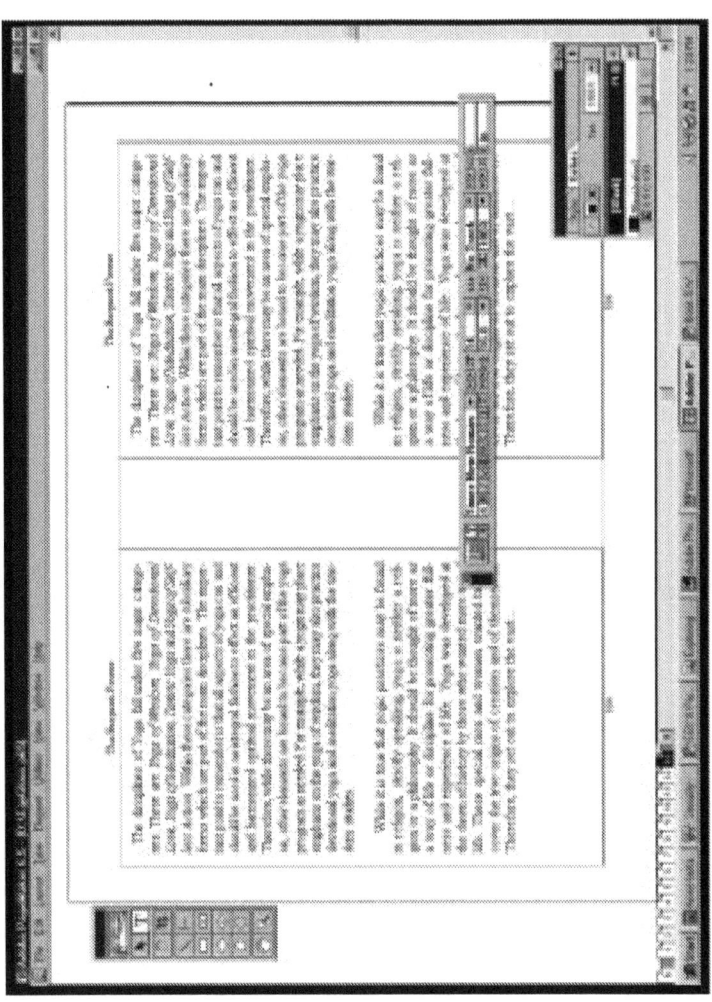

Self-Publishing

Below: Template for Cover layout using the Adobe PhotoShop program.

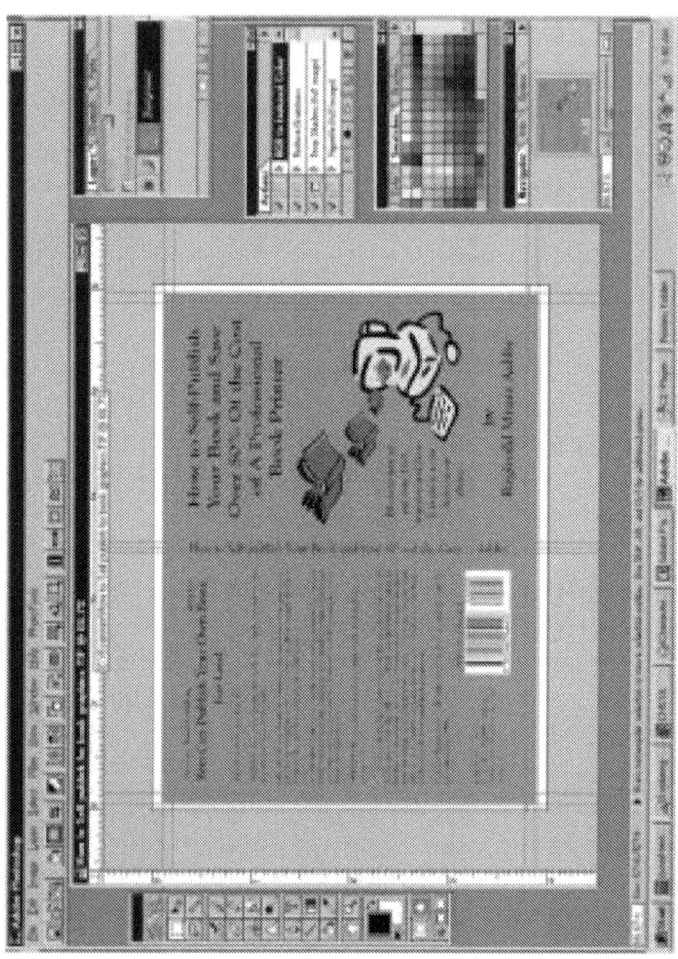

Self-Publishing

Below: Template for 24-page Catalog layout using the Microsoft Publisher program.

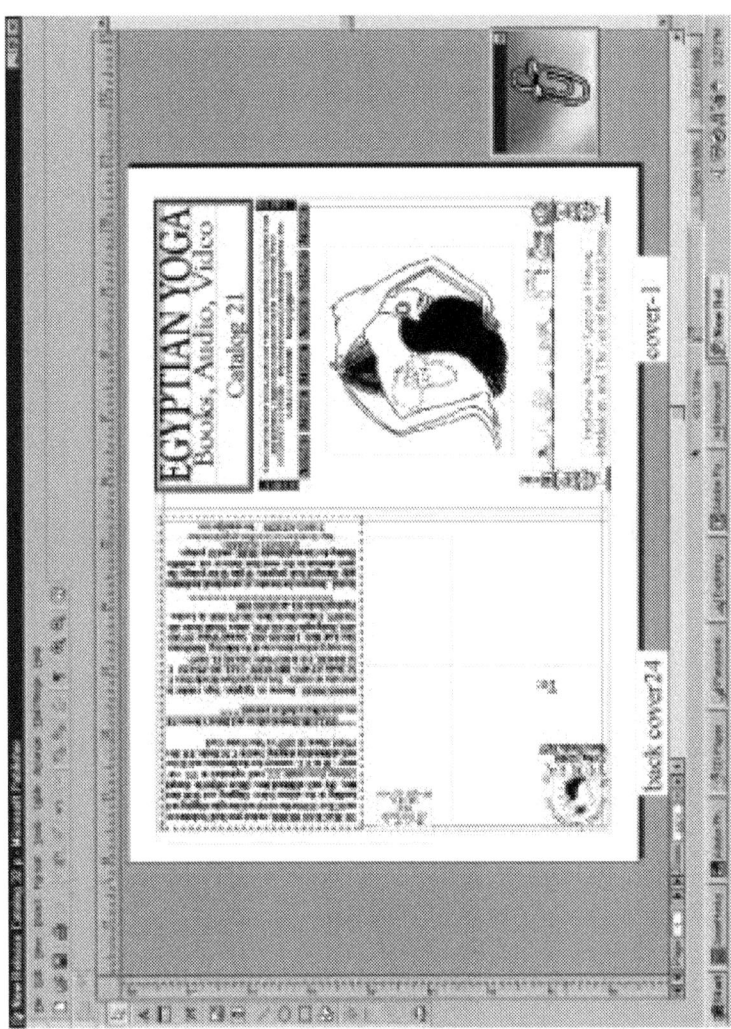

Self-Publishing

The Press Release

While you are completing your book production or shortly after the production, you will want to approach bookstores and distributors in order to let them know about the new book. An actual copy of the book is the best advertisement. It is appropriate to send one to every potential distributor you want to approach. You can find additional book distributor listings at your local library. Sending one copy of the book to each bookstore would be very costly. A press release is therefore more appropriate for the bookstores. On the following page you will see a sample press release. The press releases and flyers are valuable tools for promoting your work. You should take care to concisely and eloquently bring forth the virtues of your literary work. You should send these releases to everyone you know, including to the book distributors and bookstores. Many distributors will allow you to send them flyers that they will include with their mailings to their own bookstore customers. These flyers must meet the required specification. So check with them individually. This is a great way to inexpensively promote your books.

Self-Publishing

It can be expensive to do mailings to individuals. You may consider placing advertisements in the distributor catalogs and doing "cooperative mailings" where distributors send out the flyers for many publishers at the same time. You must supply the flyers, and sometimes there is a fee for this service. However, the mailings go to a target market, the people who buy the books. This will allow you to make every advertising dollar count.

Self-Publishing

Other Resources And References

The following books are invaluable aids to getting your book out into the marketplace, and then sold.

Publishers Marketing Association
627 Aviation Way, Manhattan Beach, Ca 90266

The Self Publishing Manual by Dan Pointer

Published by Para Publishing
P.O. Box 2206
Santa Barbara, Ca. 93118-2206

The African American Writers Survival Manual by LaRita Booth Pryor

Published by Longwood Academic, a Division of Hollowbrook Communications, Inc
Wakefield, New Hampshire, 03 872-0757

Self-Publishing

To obtain an ISBN number contact:

ABI Department of R.R Bowker Co. (908) 464-6800 or (800) 521-8110. You will use the "Advance Book Information" Form.

Self-Publishing

To Copyright your book contact the Register of Copyrights, Library of Congress, Washington DC 20559 and request Form TX and any other pertinent forms.

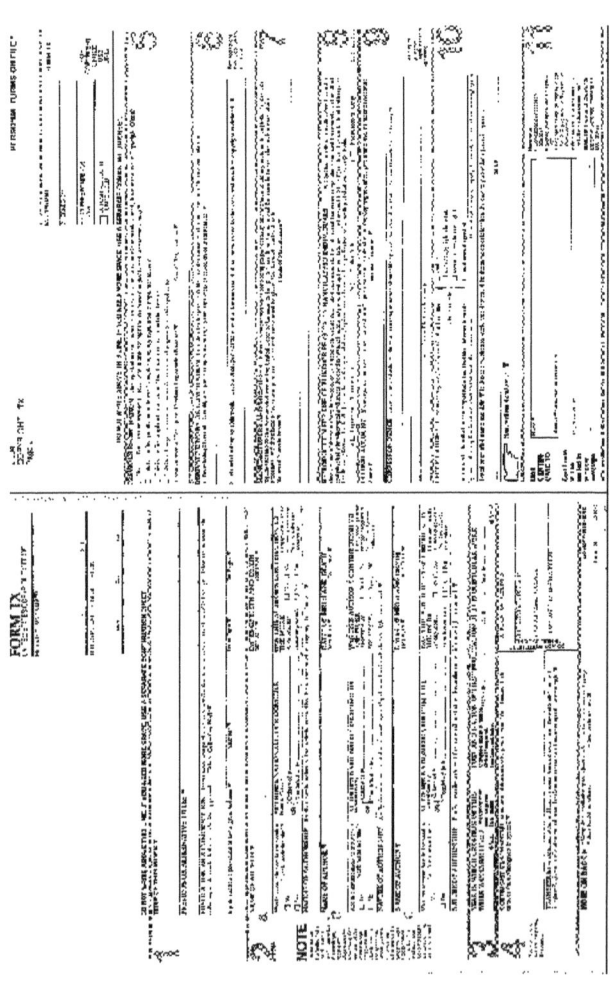

Self-Publishing

NOTES

You should keep track of the people you will do business with and make sure you keep in contact with them and establish a good working relationship. Use this section to record your local and out of town resources, the companies which you will do business with.

Company Name: _____
Address: _____
City: _____ State: _____ Zip: _____

Telephone_____
Person to contact there _____

Company Name: _____
Address: _____
City: _____ State: _____ Zip: _____

Telephone_____
Person to contact there _____

Company
Name:_____
Address: _____
City: _____ State: _____ Zip: _____

Telephone_____
Person to contact there _____

Self-Publishing

Company Name:_____
Address: _____
City: _____ State: _____ Zip: _____

Telephone_____
Person to contact there _____

Company Name:_____
Address: _____
City: _____ State: _____ Zip: _____

Telephone_____
Person to contact there _____

Company Name:_____
Address: _____
City: _____ State: _____ Zip: _____

Telephone_____
Person to contact there _____

Company Name:_____
Address: _____
City: _____ State: _____ Zip: _____

Telephone_____
Person to contact there _____

Self-Publishing

Company Name:_____
Address: _____
City: _____ State: _____ Zip: _____

Telephone_____
Person to contact there _____

Company Name:_____
Address: _____
City: _____ State: _____ Zip: _____

Telephone_____
Person to contact there _____

Company Name:_____
Address: _____
City: _____ State: _____ Zip: _____

Telephone_____
Person to contact there _____

Company Name:_____
Address: _____
City: _____ State: _____ Zip: _____

Telephone_____
Person to contact there _____

Self-Publishing

NOTES

Use this section to make notes on your book projects, setup specifications and anything else you need to keep in mind as you develop your projects.

Self-Publishing

NOTES

0Use this section to make notes on your book projects, setup specifications and anything else you need to keep in mind as you develop your projects.

Self-Publishing

NOTES

0Use this section to make notes on your book projects, setup specifications and anything else you need to keep in mind as you develop your projects.

Self-Publishing

NOTES

Use this section to make notes and drawings with the measurements for your books so that you may have a quick reference.

Self-Publishing

NOTES

Use this section to make notes and drawingswith the measurements for your books so that you may have a quick reference.

Self-Publishing

NOTES

Use this section to make notes and drawings with the measurements for your books so that you may have a quick reference.

Self-Publishing **Now Available**

Audio Cassette Lecture from Dr. Ashby on Introduction to Self-publishing

3011 Spiritual Self-Publishing

Sema Institute of Yoga/Cruzian Mystic Books P. O. Box 570459
Miami, Florida, 33257
(305) 378-6253 Fax: (305) 378-6253

AUDIO CASSETTE

Self-Publishing

To sell your books to libraries you need a Library of Congress number. Contact: Library of Congress (202) 707-6372.

You will use the "Request for Preassignment of LCC Number" Form.

Library of Congress application Form 607-7

Self-Publishing

UPDATE 2006

Greetings,

There are some exciting developments in the Self-Publishing field. For many years it has been a sort of "Holy Grail" of sorts to develop a system that could allow a publisher or writer to have a book printed without having to print thousands to get a low price and then need to keep inventories of books in a closet or a garage until they sell.

A few years ago some machines were designed to do just that but the system had some kinks and it was expensive. One of the earliest companies to develop the system into a viable organized process that incorporates the distribution of books is Lightningsource. They are associated with Ingram distribution which is one of the biggest if not the biggest distributor to regular book stores such as Barnes & Noble and Borders. They have been referred to as the "Microsoft" of POD "Print On Demand."

In 2004-2005 Amazon got in the game by buying a smaller company competing with Lightningsource called Booksurge. Booksurge produces the books in the same way and is cheaper and they are available to bookstores but the big thing is the Amazon distribution and through their own web page. The competition has reduced the cost so it is competitive with the older (commercial copying) method described in this book.

The benefits are:
- never needing to keep inventories
- you can order for yourself whenever you need to
- you can drop ship- have both send to your customers directly
- they both print in the United Kingdom, Booksurge prints in UK and Australia.
- Books never go out of print
- With Booksurge you can tie in your web page to their so

Self-Publishing

after seeing the books you can direct customers to their web page to purchase the books

If you use this system your books will be automatically available on Amazon.dom (Booksurge) and Barnes and Noble and Ingram (Lightningsource)

Web Site links:

www.Lighningsource.com
www.Booksurge.com

The procedures in this book may be adjusted as follows:

The book preparation procedures are simplified. For the smaller books you do not need to prepare 2-up pages, just one to the trim size of the final book. Save as (Adobe) pdf file and send to the printer. The cover is prepared the same way but with the dimensions the printers provide. Lightningsource has a free feature for preparing the cover. You provide the book size and number of pages at their web site and they will email you the cover template within 5 minutes.

One more note: the program Pagemaker is no longer produced. Adobe now makes a program called "Indesign". That is a very high end program and it is very expensive and takes some time to learn. If you get that program you do not need to get Adobe Acrobat to make PDF files to give to the printer.

If you use a program like Microsoft Word, Publisher or Wordperfect you will need the Acrobat program.

Self-Publishing Order Form

Telephone orders: Call (305) 378-6253. Have your AMEX, Optima, Discover, Visa or MasterCard ready.

Fax orders: (305) 378-6253

Postal Orders: C. M. Books, P.O. Box 570459, Miami, Fl. 33257. USA.

Please send the following books and / or tapes.

ITEM

_____ Cost $_____
_____ Cost $_____
_____ Cost $_____
_____ Cost $_____

Total $_____

Name: -

Address: - --
(Physical Address Please)

City: _____ State: _____ Zip:

Sales tax:
Please add 6.5% for books shipped to Florida addresses

Shipping-.
Air Mail: $6.50 first item and $.50 for each additional

-------- Payment: --
------- Check ---
Please include your Drivers license number if you are paying by check.

-------- Credit card: -------- Visa, --------- MasterCard, -------- Optima, --------
AMEX, ----------Discover

Card number: --

Name on card: _____ ___ Exp. date: _____ /

Copyright 1997-2002 Dr. Reginald Muata Ashby
C. M. book Publishing P.O.Box 570459 Miami, Florida, 33257
(305) 378-6253

www.ingramcontent.com/pod-product-compliance
Ingram Content Group UK Ltd.
Pitfield, Milton Keynes, MK11 3LW, UK
UKHW041419180426
11947UKWH00007B/209